BUSINESS *ENT*

CUSTOMER MARKETING

How to Improve the Profitability of Your Customer Base

Jay Curry
Wil Wurtz
Guido Thys
Conny Zijlstra

Published in
association with

**The Royal Bank
of Scotland**

**KOGAN
PAGE**

YOURS TO HAVE AND TO HOLD

BUT NOT TO COPY

First published in 1998

Kogan Page Limited
120 Pentonville Road
London N1 9JN

British Library Cataloguing in Publication Data

A CIP record for this book is available from the British Library.

ISBN 0 7494 2627 6

Typeset by JS Typesetting, Wellingborough, Northants.
Printed in England by Clays Ltd, St Ives plc.

Big response
to small business needs

What makes the Royal Bank of Scotland stand out when it comes to setting up your own business?

. . . .

When you're setting up your own business, choosing a bank is one of many major decisions you have to make and it's important to get it right. In an ideal world, your bank manager will understand both your immediate needs as well as your long-term objectives, support you as your business grows and help you to make the right decisions at critical times.

Following extensive research among its customers, The Royal Bank of Scotland has developed a unique, tailored service reflecting these principles for people who are just starting out or already run a small business. 'We asked a wide range of businesses what they wanted from a bank, evaluated their comments and then we used them to redefine our service,' says Ian Henderson, head of business marketing with the Royal Bank.

Twice-nominated Small Business Bank of the Year, the Royal Bank remains a clear leader in customer service. Other accolades include being chosen as one of the two top banks in the UK for franchise finance and, in two independent surveys of banks and building societies, it was the only high street bank in the top category for customer service.

RELATIONSHIP

So what makes the Royal Bank stand out? One unique feature is its team of dedicated business relationship managers who have sole responsibility for start-ups and smaller owner-managed business customers.

'One complaint against banks in the past was lack of continuity – customers got to know their manager only to find that after a short time he or she had to move on,' says Ian Henderson. 'Business relationship managers are in place for a minimum of four years to provide the continuity that customers want and have the time to give them their undivided attention. Their performance is measured according to the quality of service offered to customers.'

Business relationship managers are locally based but freed from the supervisory and administrative role of a branch manager. As a result, they focus solely on customer needs and often spend more time on their customers' premises than behind their own desks. 'The aim is to get an understanding of each business and its potential, something that is particularly relevant to people setting up their own business,' says Ian Henderson.

Every small business has its own special needs but the Royal Bank also recognises that certain specialist areas may need extra support. For example, it has appointed a number of healthcare relationship managers who are dedicated to helping doctors, dentists, vets, retail chemists and others in the health business. 'This exclusive focus gives our business relationship managers a good insight into the issues and problems behind starting up a business,' says Ian Henderson. 'They are trained to understand the small business sector and bring together a whole range of specialist financial services. This means they are in a position to deliver an outstanding service to their customers by identifying and addressing their real financial needs.'

Once a business relationship manager knows a business, it is very much part of his or her job to play a pro-active role in looking after the customer. This may involve helping to maximise the return on surplus business funds or pointing out the most appropriate and cost-effective way of raising finance. In addition, they are equipped to provide rapid responses to customers' financial requirements with lending decisions guaranteed within 48 hours.

INNOVATIVE

The Royal Bank is always on the look-out for new and innovative services to meet the needs of today's ever-changing business environment. Royline, the bank's sophisticated electronic banking system, has been upgraded to keep pace with the latest technological developments, with a Windows version now available.

In addition, we have developed a business plan software package which takes the hassle out of writing a business plan. The package will ask you a series of questions about yourself, your idea and your business intentions. All you have to do is type in the answers and the package will produce a draft business plan.

For new businesses, this start-up pack is available either from local branches or by calling freephone 0800 521607.

'Every big business was once a small business. They are the wealth creators of tomorrow and we want to help as many as possible to turn into bigger businesses by providing them with all the banking services they need to achieve that goal,' says Ian Henderson. 'Over the year, the Royal Bank has helped thousands of companies do just that, underlining its recognition of the importance of start-up and owner-managed businesses to the well-being of the economy. We now operate what we believe to be the most far-reaching customer service programme in British banking. Based on our conviction that quality of services is the key to fostering strong and enduring relationships with all our customers. 'The result so far, both from start-up businesses and those that have been in existence for some time, is that this approach is what our customers want and, even more important for them, it really works.'

Contents

Acknowledgements

The authors wish to thank the following people and organizations involved in the creation of this book.

- Our families and friends who have given us so much support (and by now want to scream when they hear the words 'customer marketing').
- Our hard-working – and ever questioning – Associates who have taught us that there is no monopoly on good ideas.
- Our ACUMAP consortium colleagues at PTT Telecom, Telecom Italia, Databank and the European Commission.
- Our clients, from whom we have learned so much.

The Partners of MSP Associates

Jay Curry
Wil Wurt
Guido Thys
Conny Zijlstra

Amsterdam

Special notice

The European Commission has supported the development of customer marketing through an ESPRIT programme grant to Project ACUMAP – **A C**ustomer **M**arketing **P**ilot – operated by a consortium consisting of PTT Telecom, Telecom Italia, Databank SpA and MSP Associates.

A keygoal of Project ACUMAP is to refine the customer marketing methodology, tools and training materials and to make them available for any European company which wants to improve its competitive position.

The book you now have in your hand is a by-product of Project ACUMAP.

For more information about customer marketing tools, software and materials please contact:

MSP Associates, Oranje Nassaulaan 35, 1075 AJ Amsterdam, The Netherlands, tel: +31-20-679-3077 fax: +31-20-679-2224 email: info@mspa.nl

or visit the website: www.customermarketing.n/

Foreword

SHOULD YOU BE READING THIS BOOK?

Here are three questions to help you decide whether or not to continue reading this book.

1. How much did you spend last year on marketing and sales?
2. What was your return on that investment: 12 per cent?. . . 22 per cent?. . . 77 per cent? How can you improve on it next year?
3. How can you get marketing and sales to work together more efficiently?

If you have ready answers to these questions, then please return this book to the bookstore or give it to a less fortunate colleague because you do not need it. But if you want to know how to measure, manage and improve your investments in marketing budgets and sales salaries, then this could be the book for you. Read on to find out for sure!

Part I

Customer Marketing:
What's in it for you?

Marketing and Sales: A 'Black Box'

Would you be fired if you made these statements to your top management, board of directors or shareholders?

- 'I know that 50 per cent of my production is rejected. But I don't know why.'
- 'I know that 50 per cent of my deliveries are late. But I can't do anything about it.'
- 'I know that 50 per cent of my administration is inaccurate. What a pity.'

Admit it: these statements would result in no time in your being downsized or appointed 'Manager of Special Projects' in Iceland. But would your career be damaged if you made this statement?

- 'I know that 50 per cent of my advertising budget is wasted. The problem is I don't know which 50 per cent.'

Probably not. The man who said this – Mr Lever, a founder of Unilever – was anointed as Lord Leverhulme. Today his words are still acceptable to top management, the board of directors and shareholders. Why? Simply because, for many companies, marketing and sales is a 'black box'; a budgetary 'Bermuda Triangle' into which large amounts of money are poured without the rigorous process control techniques used to measure and manage the productivity of production, and of logistic and administrative processes. Here are some examples of the 'black box' syndrome that we have encountered in our consulting practice.

- Company A, which normally spends months to calculate the return on investment (ROI) prior to purchasing a £31,250 production machine, approves a £625,000 advertising campaign in an afternoon.
- Company B, with a sophisticated just-in-time (JIT) logistics flow to manage components costing £31 each, has no system to track field sales force visits which cost £62 each.
- Company C has a perfect invoicing system for billing customers. But it has no idea of how satisfied these customers are with the products and service invoiced.

How is it possible for these situations to exist? There are two main reasons.

- Many people subscribe to the conventional wisdom that marketing and sales are 'intuitive' processes which do not lend themselves to measurement.
- The traditional organizational and budgetary split between the marketing and sales departments. In the real world – that is in the perception of the customer – marketing and sales are interrelated. The customer assumes that the salesperson and the sales brochure come from the same source. In fact, these two customer contacts are charged to two very different budgets, managed by two very different people – the sales manager and the marketing manager – who are usually separated by a huge emotional divide.

Given this situation, calculating the ROI of the salesperson, armed with the brochure, is virtually impossible.

In this book, we will attempt to show you how marketing and sales can work together to apply statistical process control (SPC) techniques – the cybernetic loop of data registration, analysis, planning and realization – to the marketing and sales processes. This book will also help you to apply these techniques where it matters most: at the customer level. Ultimately, both the marketing and the sales departments are responsible for influencing the behaviour of (potential) customers by:

- identifying suitable prospects from a list of 'possibles'
- creating new customers

- re-establishing contact with past customers
- keeping customers who have reached the top of their spending levels
- upgrading customers where the company's 'share of customer' can be improved.

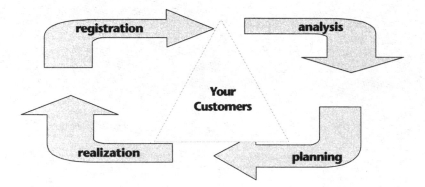

Figure 1.1 *Applying process control for marketing and sales, where it all happens: your customers*

Where it all Happens: Your Customers

Your company's revenues, profits and market share – and your salary – come ultimately from only one source: your customers. No matter what products and services you provide – be it confectionery, computers, insurance or temporary help – customers are the heart of your business. When you get right down to it, the one single thing a company needs to be in business is a customer!

You do not need money to be in business; you do not need to have an idea to be in business; you do not need a store, factory or office location to be in business; you do not need personnel to be in business; you do not even need a product or service to be in business. All these things help, of course, but without a customer, you are not in business. If you have just one customer, you are in business. If you have a lot of good customers, you have a successful business. If your company is successful – and we hope it is – we are sure that you have developed a solid base of good customers who do good things such as the following.

● *Buy more from you even if your prices are (somewhat) higher than the competition*. Obviously you cannot gouge people and expect to get away with it; but think about that small grocery store or speciality clothing store where they know your name or the service is pleasant. Sure, you pay a bit more but you keep coming back. Your customers will treat you the same way if you do to them as you would have them do to you.

- *Recommend you to colleagues, family, friends.* There is no better promotional message than a recommendation from a satisfied customer. People talk about their experiences with suppliers – both good and bad. A recent study showed that information technology (IT) managers rate advice from colleagues as one of the most important sources of information when buying a system; and that more than 60 per cent of IT managers give advice privately to colleagues outside their own organization. Imagine: the IT manager of Procter & Gamble meets the IT manager of Kimberly-Clark at a computer conference. They do not talk about nappies. They talk about who is doing what to whom in the IT community; and their experiences, good and bad, with suppliers.

  While a good customer will generate a lot of business for you, a dissatisfied customer can hurt you badly. It has been said that: 'For every complaint there are ten others who didn't make the effort to tell you of their dissatisfaction. And since every dissatisfied customer gripes to an average of six people, every complaint represents 60 people who are walking around with a negative image of your company'.

- *Make you the 'standard' for the organization or family.* What could be better than having the boss at your customer site sending out a memo to all employees: 'All (name your product or service) must be ordered from (the name of your company)'. Good customers write memos like that.

- *Try out your new products and help you to make them better.* Good customers are usually willing to invest their time and effort to help you develop and improve your (new) products and services. In the case of mainframe computers and sophisticated technology, customer involvement in research and development of new products can be worth tens of thousands of pounds or more in man-hours and expertise. The beauty is that as customers become involved in your business, they tend to become better customers.

- *Use your support, service and other facilities.* Service, support, training, add-ons. These often highly profitable products and services are usually offered to customers with whom you have a good relationship.

Since customers are the crux of your business, it is essential to understand who they are and what they do. One way to view and analyse your customers is by using a 'customer pyramid'.

Customer Pyramids

A customer pyramid is a useful tool to help you visualize and analyse the behaviour of your customers and to make plans to improve that behaviour. You can also use a customer pyramid to create more customer awareness among managers and staff in your company. Replace the sterile monthly sales charts on the company cafeteria walls with customer pyramids that graphically illustrate what is really happening each month: the up–down/in–out behaviour of your customers. The basic elements of a customer pyramid are shown in Figure 3.1.

Figure 3.1 The basic elements of a customer pyramid

- *Active customers* – persons or companies which have purchased goods or services from your company within a given period, say the last 12 months.

- *Inactive customers* – persons or companies which have purchased goods or services from your company in the past, but
  not within the given period. Inactive customers are an
  important source of potential revenue; and also a source of
  information about what you need to do to prevent your
  active customers from becoming inactive customers!
- *Prospects* – persons or companies with whom you have some
  kind of relationship but they have not yet purchased any
  goods or services, for example, people who have responded
  to a mailing and requested your brochure; companies which
  have issued you a Request for Bid; contacts met at a trade
  fair, etc. Prospects are persons and companies whom you
  expect to achieve active customer status in the near future.
- *Suspects* – persons or companies which you could serve with
  your products and services but you do not yet have a relationship with them. Normally you seek to begin a relationship
  with suspects and qualify them as prospects, with the longer-
  term goal of converting them to active customers.
- *The rest of the world* – persons or companies which simply
  have no need or desire to purchase or use your products and
  services. You will never make any money from this group,
  however, it is important to be able to visualize the group to
  understand how much marketing time and money are spent
  trying to communicate with these people and companies.

The real value of the customer pyramid becomes evident when
you segment your active customers into categories of behaviour
critical to the success of your company, such as sales revenue.
For most companies we recommend a 'standard' customer
pyramid which is formed by clustering customers according to
four categories of sales revenues – 'top', 'big', 'medium' and
'small' – as shown in Figure 3.2.

To create this customer pyramid, make a list of your customers
with their sales revenues for a given period (normally your last
fiscal year). This information should be available in your
accounts department. Then sort the customers and list them
from top to bottom, beginning with the largest customer in
terms of sales and ending with the smallest customer. (A spreadsheet program such as Excel or Lotus 1-2-3 makes this task more
manageable.) The result is a 'customer sort' from which you
can segment the list of customers into four categories.

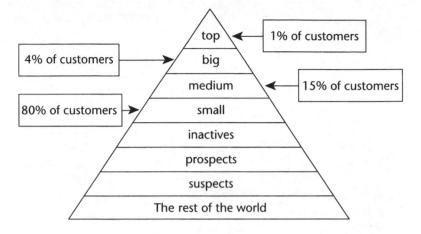

Figure 3.2 *'Standard' customer pyramid (sales revenues)*

- *'Top' customers* – the top 1 per cent of your active customers in terms of sales revenues. (If you have 1000 active customers, your 'top' customers would be the first ten customers on your list.)
- *'Big' customers* – the next 4 per cent of your active customers in terms of sales revenues. (If you have 1000 active customers, your 'big' customers would be the next 40 customers on your list.)
- *'Medium' customers* – the next 15 per cent of your active customers in terms of sales revenues. (If you have 1000 active customers, your 'medium' customers would be the next 150 customers on your list.)
- *'Small' Customers* – the remaining 80 per cent of your active customers in terms of sales revenues. (If you have 1000 active customers, your 'small' customers would be the remaining 800 customers on your list.)

To complete your customer pyramid, add the number of inactive customers (also found from your accounting records); your active prospects (ask the sales department); and your suspects (ask the marketing department). Do not worry yet about the rest of the world.

Figure 3.3 is an example of a customer pyramid for the 'InterTech' company which has 450 active customers. Thus InterTech has four 'top', 18 'big', 68 'medium' and 360 'small' customers. Notice also the customer pyramid segment 'boundaries', which will become evident from your customer sort. For

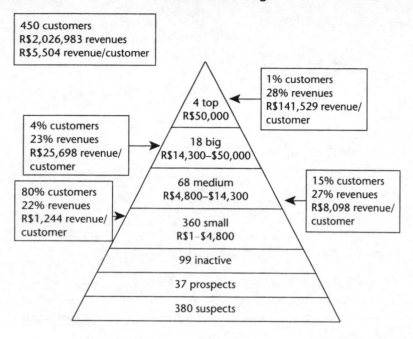

Figure 3.3 *InterTech customer pyramid*

InterTech, 'top' customers spend more than R$50,000; 'big' customers spend between R$14,300 and R$50,000; 'medium' customers spend between R$4800 and R$14,300; and 'small' customers spend from R$1 to R$4800. (We will return to the InterTech case in Part II of this book.)

Some companies and industries find it more practical or useful to work with a customer pyramid based on behaviour other than sales revenues. For instance, the financial industry (banks and insurance) can segment customers based on the number of products or product clusters purchased or used by each customer, ie the 'one shots' – often 80 per cent or more of a bank or insurance company's customers – have only one account or insurance policy; 'duets' have two; 'triples' three; and the 'top' have four. For many retail organizations, the number of visits per customer is a key – and measurable – factor. For food stores, the number of visits per month are important. For others, such as clothing stores and hairdressers, the number of visits per year are used to build a customer pyramid. Companies which sell capital goods such as machines, trucks, motor vehicles, etc may prefer to work with a customer pyramid based on the number of consecutive purchases made by a customer

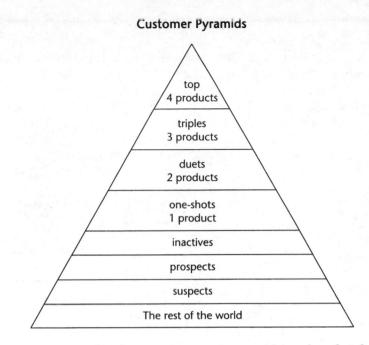

Figure 3.4 *Banking/insurance customer pyramid (number of products per customer)*

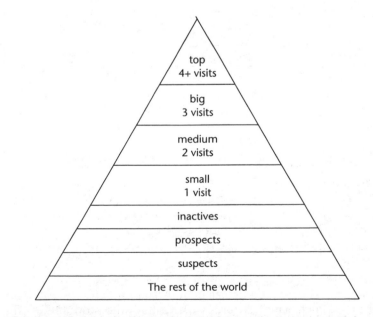

Figure 3.5 *Retail customer pyramid (store visits per month/year)*

over a long period of time. For example, a car dealer would count a customer who has purchased four or more vehicles over the period as a 'top' customer; the customer who has purchased three as a 'triple'; and so on. As many capital goods suppliers also sell services and 'consumables', they often find that a customer pyramid based on yearly gross margin (sales revenues less costs of goods and services) may be even more useful.

Figure 3.6 *Capital goods customer pyramid (number of consecutive purchases)*

MULTIPLE CUSTOMER PYRAMIDS

Many marketing and sales executives have no problem answering the question, 'Who is your customer?' The retailer knows his customer comes into the store. The temporary help agency counts the personnel department as its customer. The insurance broker sells either to private individuals or to a corporate decision-making unit.

However, defining the customer is not always so simple. For example, if you are a food processor with branded product, who is the customer? The distributor which buys the product directly from you? The supermarket which buys from the distributor?

Or the individual shopper who buys from the supermarket? Similarly, who is the customer for a producer of prescription drugs? The drug wholesaler which purchases the product from the drug company and sells it to the pharmacy or chemist? The pharmacy or chemist which sells the product to the patient? The patient who buys the product from the pharmacy or chemist? The doctor who writes the prescription for the drug? Or the insurance company which reimburses the patient?

Two guidelines help you to define your customers and your customer pyramids.

1. *Make pyramids for those customers whose behaviour you can influence.* It does not make sense to spend a lot of time tracking companies or individuals in the 'food chain' over which you have no influence. Therefore, a prescription drug company may have a customer pyramid only for the prescribing doctor who is visited by the 'detail person'. However, a food processor may have customer pyramids for the distributor, the supermarkets and individual households.
2. *Make pyramids for customers requiring different marketing and sales methods.* You may have a product which you sell to end users and to distributors or dealers. If you have split your sales force into direct and indirect business units, you may find it useful to make completely different pyramids for each business unit in order to make performance comparisons and for differences in customer (contact) plans.

Ten Lessons Learnt from Customer Pyramids

The concept of customer marketing and the customer pyramid as a tool to visualize and analyse customer behaviour was introduced in 1988. Since then, we have built and looked at hundreds of customer pyramids of companies in a wide variety of industries: electronic component manufacturers; wholesalers; car dealers; retailers; manufacturers of fast moving consumer goods; banks and insurers; even law firms! While these companies were wildly different in terms of size and types of business, their customer pyramids reflected remarkably similar patterns of customer behaviour. The ways in which all these companies interacted with their customers was also remarkably similar. From our experiences with these companies we are able to distil and share with you ten lessons learned from customer pyramids.

To illustrate these ten lessons, we will use as a case 'General Casualty Company (GCC)', a regional insurance company in, say, Ruritania. After all, every reader of this book is a customer of at least one insurance company – probably three or more! While GCC obviously does not exist, the customer pyramids have been developed through familiarity with the customer pyramids of more than 12 insurance companies and brokers. Just to set the background, here is some basic data on GCC, with monetary amounts in Ruritanian dollars (R$).

- 155,592 customers
- 1.27 policies per customer

- R$50,042,464 premium revenues
- R$7,104,957 operational profit
- R$322 premium revenue per customer
- R$46 operational profit per customer

Figure 4.1 is the GCC customer pyramid, which shows the customer base segmented by number of policies per customer which also – for the sake of clarity – resulted in pyramid segments showing 1 per cent, 4 per cent, 15 per cent and 80 per cent of customers. You will probably want to compare this with your own customer pyramid and activities to see which, if any, of the ten lessons apply to your situation.

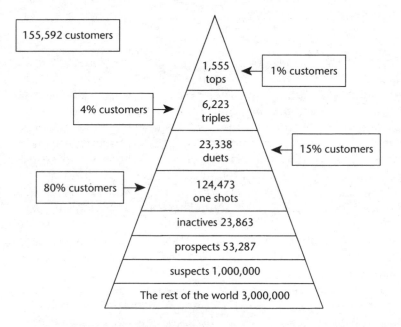

Figure 4.1 *GCC customer pyramid*

1. THE TOP 20 PER CENT OF THE CUSTOMERS DELIVER 80 PER CENT OF REVENUES

Just about every customer pyramid we have ever constructed or seen proves the validity of the 80/20 Pareto principle. There are of course some variances, from 80/30 to 80/10. But the revenue analysis is almost always in the 80/20 area. The revenue

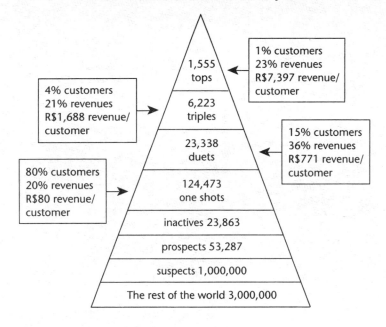

Figure 4.2 *The 80/20 Pareto principle*

distribution of GCC is also quite normal, ie revenue contribution per customer segment does not vary greatly (see Figure 4.2). There are exceptions: some business-to-business companies derive a great deal of revenue from a very small number of customers. The customer pyramid sometimes reveals this vulnerability.

We once presented a customer pyramid to 500 employees of an IT company which showed that 1 per cent of their customers – 16 in number – were good for 49 per cent of revenue. The customer pyramid demonstrated with facts and figures that the departure of just one of these customers could mean bankruptcy. The 'customer care' attitude of these employees improved quite quickly as a result of the presentation.

2. THE TOP 20 PER CENT OF THE CUSTOMERS DELIVER MORE THAN 100 PER CENT OF PROFITS

Now you can understand why all airline companies have 'frequent flyer' programmes – a relatively small percentage of their passengers deliver all the profits, and more. Put another way,

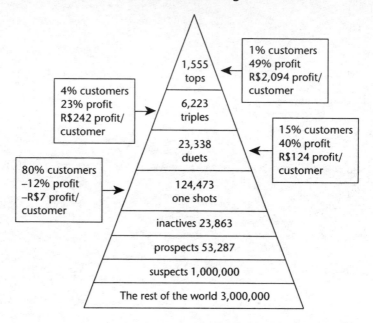

Figure 4.3 *20 per cent of customers deliver more than 100 per cent of profits*

airlines – like most companies – lose money on 80 per cent of their customers!

If you fairly allocate all costs – product, overheads and marketing/sales – spent on each customer or customer segment in the customer pyramid, you will probably discover that this amazing fact of business life holds true for you as well. For example, take the average revenue of your small customers; then deduct the cost of product or services to arrive at the gross margin per small customer. If you then deduct the cost per company for invoicing, customer service and one or two sales visits at £93 each, then there is not much contribution, if any, left over for the shareholders. With the GCC example (Figure 4.1), small customers deliver an average of R$80 in revenues. The cost of invoicing and collecting premiums alone eats up the margin for these customers. (Later on in this book we will discuss how 'customer based accounting' techniques can help you to measure the profitability of the customers in your pyramid.)

3. EXISTING CUSTOMERS DELIVER UP TO 90 PER CENT OF REVENUES

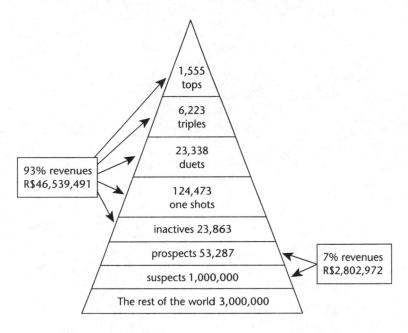

Figure 4.4 *Existing customers deliver 90 per cent of revenues*

This is probably the most profound lesson to be learned from customer pyramids because it drives home the fact of life that companies can only stay in business with a base of customers (Figure 4.4). Even companies only two years old often get 60–70 per cent of their revenues from existing customers. Yet most managers I talk to are not conscious of the fact that 90 per cent of their business comes from current customers.

We were once challenged at a seminar by an executive whose business was moving industrial plants from one country to another. He said that his service was a once in a lifetime deal for his customers: he had virtually no customers that moved a plant more than once, and thus had no repeat business. However, on questioning, he revealed that his real 'customers' were a handful of engineers who managed plant relocation projects. These engineers were good for about 80 per cent of his revenues. In short, this lesson underscores this statement made by Peter Drucker: 'The business of a company is making and keeping customers'.

4. THE BULK OF MARKETING BUDGETS IS OFTEN SPENT ON NON-CUSTOMERS

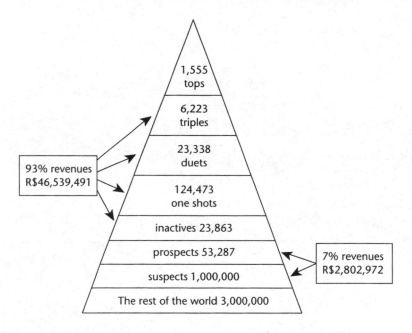

Figure 4.5 *Bulk of marketing budgets spent on non-customers*

Although every company gets about 90 per cent of its revenue from existing customers, most companies spend as much as 60–80 per cent of their marketing money in communicating with non-customers (Figure 4.5). Of course it takes much more time, effort and money to make a sale to a non-customer than a customer. Why? Because a sale to a non-customer means the creation of a customer. And customer creation often requires a lot of persuasion, not just to sell the product or service, but to overcome the doubts and fears which prospects and suspects have when considering whether or not to spend money with a new supplier.

The problem is that a great deal of the marketing budget spent on non-customers is often wasted on 'the rest of the world'. Take nappies, for example. TV advertisements for nappies run during prime time and are seen by 100 per cent of all households watching television. But of these households, only 8 per cent have nappy-age children. Thus there is a guaranteed waste of 92 per cent of the television budget which is targeted at 'the rest of the world'.

The focus on non-customers also has a psychological element. Marketing and sales people often get a bigger kick from getting 'new business' than taking a routine order from an old, familiar and faithful customer. However, we will see why more attention paid to some existing customers can deliver a dramatic growth in profits.

5. 5–30 PER CENT OF ALL CUSTOMERS HAVE A POTENTIAL FOR UPGRADING IN THE CUSTOMER PYRAMID

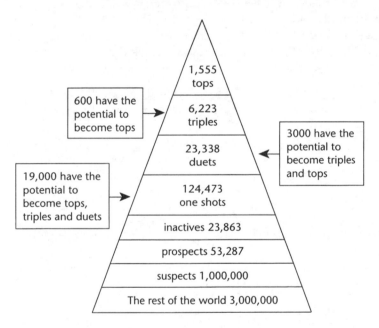

Figure 4.6 *Potential for upgrading customers*

While most companies lose money on their 'small' customers, this should not lead to a wholesale purge such as sending them off to the competition or turning them over to dealers and distributors. Twenty per cent of revenues from 'small' customers provides a contribution to overheads and helps to build economies of scale. More importantly, a number of small customers have the potential to move quickly to the top of the pyramid (Figure 4.6). Not necessarily because their needs for your products and services will increase dramatically, but because your 'share of customer' is low. In other words, the 'small' customer in your pyramid may be a 'top' customer in the pyramid of your competitor!

The marketing manager of a computer company once confessed to me that he wanted to get rid of all customers who spent less than £3,125 per year. But he changed his mind when, making his customer pyramid, he discovered that one of his 'small' customers was KLM, the airline company which was currently spending about £62,500,000 per year on computer hardware, software and services.

It is not just 'small' customers that can be upgraded. A number of your 'medium' and 'big' customers may have a need for additional products and services which you offer but as yet you have not bothered to do any cross-selling. Customer upgrading also has a lot to do with customer satisfaction.

6. CUSTOMER SATISFACTION IS CRITICAL FOR MIGRATION UP THE PYRAMID

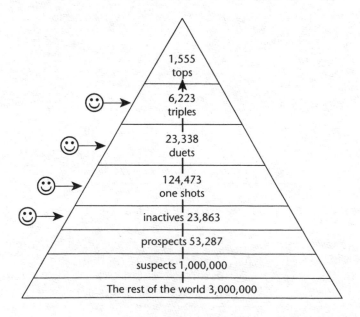

Figure 4.7 *Customer satisfaction is critical for migration up the pyramid*

We have done some studies on the relationship between customer satisfaction and customer behaviour and, without fail, there is a strong correlation between upward migration in the customer pyramid and customer satisfaction. The most comprehensive recent research on this topic was done by Jones and Sasser and published as the article 'Why satisfied customers defect', *Harvard Business Review*, December 1995. This study reveals how much customer satisfaction really pays off at the bottom line, for example 'highly satisfied' Xerox customers had a repeat sales rate of six times higher than customers who said that they were just 'satisfied'. In today's competitive environment with high production and service standards, people expect all their suppliers to perform at a satisfactory level. So if your customers tell you they are 'satisfied', watch out!

7. MARKETING AND SALES ARE RESPONSIBLE FOR INFLUENCING CUSTOMER BEHAVIOUR

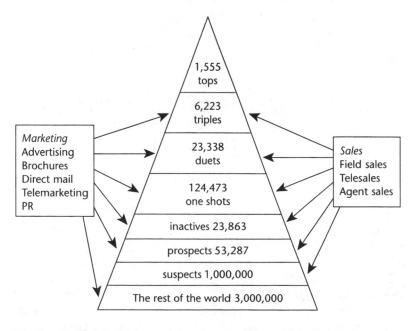

Figure 4.8 *Marketing and sales are responsible for influencing customer behaviour*

If you ask marketing and sales people what they do for a living, you will get answers like this: 'We identify and satisfy needs', 'We sell products and services', 'We develop and maintain relationships', etc. But at the end of the day, marketing and sales departments and people have the task of influencing the behaviour of (potential) customers. In marketing this can be achieved through advertising, brochures, direct mail, tele-marketing and PR; and in sales through field sales, telesales and agent sales. Marketing and sales people are charged with the heavy responsibility of:

- identifying (qualified) prospects from a pool of suspects, eliminating from consideration, when possible, 'the rest of the world'
- creating new customers
- reactivating inactive customers
- keeping those customers who have reached the top of their spending levels
- upgrading customers where the company's 'share of customer' can be improved.

However, marketing and sales are not the only departments and people involved with customers.

8. OTHER DEPARTMENTS AND PEOPLE ALSO INFLUENCE CUSTOMER BEHAVIOUR – FOR BETTER OR WORSE

While marketing and sales may be formally tasked with influencing customer behaviour, other departments and people in the organization have a great deal of influence on customers which may exceed that of marketing and sales! Your marketing communications manager, for instance, may send out four mailings per year to customers. But another department – accounts receivable – sends that same customer a minimum of 12 very important mailings each year: the invoices! If the invoices are incorrect or hard to understand, the influence on the customer may be quite negative at that critical moment in the relationship when money must be transferred to the supplier.

Let us say that you have a new and inexperienced account manager who visits his accounts six times per year to build the relationship (and sell some product). Customer dissatisfaction by his lack of experience is more than compensated by the savvy service technician who keeps the customer happy with extra service and 'stroking' when he also shows up six times per year for maintenance calls. In short, the task of influencing customer behaviour is the task of everyone in the organization. If you accept this premiss, you need to ask yourself some critical questions about 'non marketing and sales' managers and employees.

- Do they understand the importance of customers to the health and continuity of the company?
- Are they aware of their role in identifying, creating, keeping and upgrading customers?
- Do they have the experience and know-how to play that role successfully?
- Have they access to the customer information they need?

9. A 2 PER CENT NET UPWARDS MIGRATION OF CUSTOMERS CAN RESULT IN 10 PER CENT MORE REVENUE (AND 50–100 PER CENT MORE PROFIT, IF FIXED COSTS REMAIN THE SAME)

Some of your active customers will depart, die or disappear every year. Some prospects and suspects will become new customers. Some customers will drop down in the pyramid during the year; others will move up.

The lesson of this customer pyramid shows how important it is to realize a net upwards migration of your customer base at the end of the financial year. The result will be a praiseworthy increase in revenues; and if you can keep your marketing, sales and overhead costs the same, the ensuing profit explosion will do wonders for your year-end bonus. The GCC case in Figure 4.9 shows how a 1.6 per cent net upward migration in the customer pyramid resulted in a 14 per cent revenue increase and a whopping 79 per cent jump in operational profit!

We will discuss in detail how marketing and sales budgets can be reallocated to help you realize customer upgrading by shifting funds from 'the rest of the world' to the customer base and focusing on customers with growth potential.

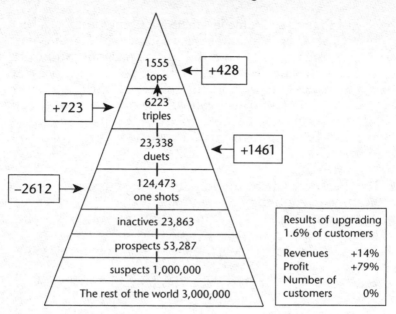

Figure 4.9 *Realizing a net upwards migration of the customer base*

10. BUSINESS SUCCESS IS A RESULT OF CUSTOMER SUCCESS

To be successful with your company – and achieve the fame, power and riches you seek – you need only focus on three things.

1. Get new customers into your pyramid.
2. Move customers higher into your pyramid.
3. Keep customers from leaving the pyramid.

The marketing and sales profitability model explains what you need to make it happen; and the customer marketing method-ology tells you how to make it happen.

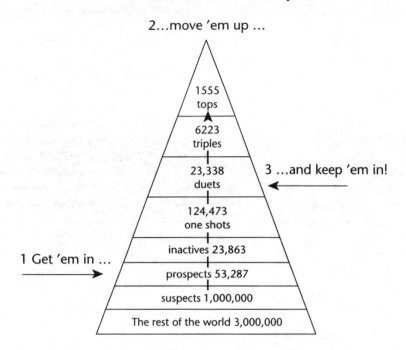

Figure 4.10 *The marketing and sales profitability model*

5

Towards A Customer-based Business Model

Conclusions drawn from observing customer behaviour and analysing customer pyramids over the years has led to development of the customer-based business with its two elements: customer performance and customer focus.

CUSTOMER PERFORMANCE FACTORS

Customer value

Profitable marketing and sales result when you have a number of customers which generate more operational profit than the operational losses incurred by doing business with the remaining customers. Customer value is not related to the gross profit or the margin of a customer alone. Marketing and sales costs play an important role in determining the value of a customer. For example, you may make money on a small or medium size customer which phones in repeat orders on a regular basis. But if you allow a salesperson to visit this customer six times a year because of an infatuation with the front desk receptionist, the value of that customer is likely to become negative.

Customer behaviour

While cost factors play an important role in the profitability of a customer, customer value is to a large extent determined by customer behaviour. Positive customer behaviour means, in the first place, that a customer is a customer, ie the customer buys from you. Customer behaviour is usually measured in terms of revenue, either monetary or volume of product or services ordered over a period of time.

A second customer behaviour factor is customer lifetime, or the average length of time as measured in months or years which the average customer does business with you.

A third and important customer behaviour factor is 'share of customer': the extent to which a customer meets his needs for the kinds of products or services by doing business with you. To illustrate 'share of customer', let us use as an example a vehicle dealer, Auto Smith. Ajax Taxi has 20 vehicles, 18 of which were bought from Auto Smith, giving Smith a 90 per cent share of customer Ajax Taxi. Mega Couriers also bought 18 vehicles from Auto Smith but these are only a fraction of his 200 vehicle fleet, giving Auto Smith only a 9 per cent share of customer Mega Couriers. The customer behaviour of Ajax Taxi is, of course, much more positive for Auto Smith than Mega Couriers.

Customer satisfaction

Happy and satisfied customers behave in a positive manner. They will buy a lot from you and will give you a large share of their business. Customer satisfaction is derived largely from the quality and reliability of your products and services. You make good on your explicit and implied promises. Recent research results have demonstrated that customers who are only just satisfied are likely to walk away for a slightly more attractive proposition from your competitor. The major goal of any customer satisfaction programme should be to achieve 'preferred supplier' status with as many customers as possible. 'Preferred supplier' status means that a customer formally or implicitly makes the policy known within the organization that, whenever possible, any purchases of goods and services in your category will be supplied by... you!

CUSTOMER FOCUS FACTORS

Customer performance – customer value, customer behaviour and customer satisfaction – is something which happens outside the company. Customer performance is to a large extent determined by customer focus factors inside the company. There are three primary and six secondary customer focus factors in this domain (Figure 5.1).

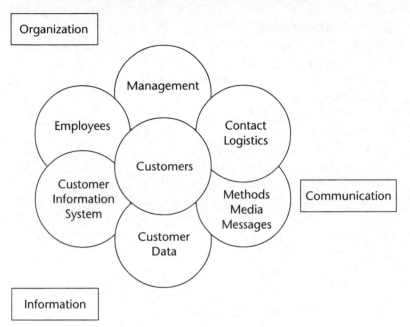

Figure 5.1 *Customer focus factors*

- Organization:
  - managers
  - employees.
- Communications:
  - contact logistics
  - methods, media, messages.
- Information:
  - customer data
  - customer information system.

Companies with positive customer focus demonstrate characteristics such as the following.

Organization

Managers are committed to customer focus; set an example; and budget time and money for customer process improvement. *Employees* have the necessary customer care skills and experience; have a customer care attitude; and work in teams to satisfy customer needs.

Communications

Contact logistics: customer communications are well planned; on time; with no sloppiness in execution. The most appropriate *methods/media/messages* are applied to each customer (segment); communications are interactive and stress customer benefits rather than product features.

Information

Customer data is relevant; complete; and up to date. *Customer information systems* are effective, flexible and user-friendly.

Merging the customer performance and customer focus factors results in the customer-based business model shown in Figure 5.2.

Figure 5.2 *A customer-based business model*

By now you probably agree that if your company scores high in customer value, customer behaviour, customer satisfaction and customer focus, you are much more likely to grow and prosper than your competitors. How can you effectively measure and manage these factors? Accountants can help you to measure profits but how about customer value, customer behaviour, customer satisfaction and customer focus?

If you ask sales managers which are their ten largest customers they may be able to name some of them. But you will search for a long time to find someone who can tell you within

24 hours the profit contribution of this top ten band of customers.

We do about 40 seminars and conferences per year, addressing about 2500 managers. Each time we ask for a show of hands to see how many work for companies which measure customer satisfaction on a structured and consistent basis. Only about 10–15 per cent of the attendees put their hands in the air. Of these, the majority only do surveys with limited samples, once every year or two!

If 90 per cent of the business comes from current customers, a constant monitoring of satisfaction levels would make sense. If the top 20 per cent of the customers deliver 80 per cent of the business, should not each and every one of these customers be surveyed on a continuing basis? In short, process control techniques – registration, analysis, planning and realization – must be added to the customer-based business model. The result is customer marketing!

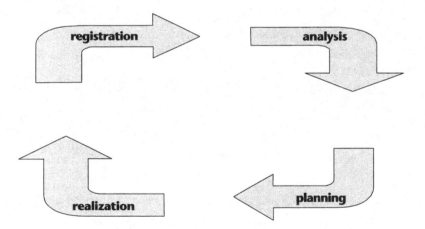

Figure 5.3 *Adding process control techniques to the customer-based business model*

6

Customer Marketing Defined

The 'official' definition of customer marketing:

> Customer marketing is a structured business methodology which uses process control techniques to realize customer goals through customer focus throughout the entire company.

The customer goals are:
- customer value
- customer behaviour
- customer satisfaction.

The customer focus factors are:
- organization
- communications
- information.

The methodology is shown in Figure 6.1.

The customer marketing methodology is carried out on a continuing basis in four phases, normally in cycles during your fiscal year.

1. *Registration* of data in the customer performance and customer focus domains.
2. *Analysis* of the data to form information for decision making and planning.

Figure 6.1 *Customer marketing methodology*

3. *Planning* customer performance and customer focus goals; and the activities to realize them.
4. *Realization* of the plans by marketing, sales, service and others with direct or indirect customer contact.

In this book we will take a look at how each customer marketing phase works in the 'real world' to see how customer marketing can turn marketing and sales into a transparent 'white box', no longer a mystery to your controller, your managing director or your shareholders! But first let us look at the characteristics of companies which have implemented the customer marketing methodology.

7

The Customer Marketing Company

Implementing customer marketing in your company may well bring about some changes, refinements and improvements in the ways in which you deal with your customers. Take time now to review these key characteristics of a customer marketing company and see how these compare with your own situation.

- You (try to) measure and improve the performance of every customer.
- You (try to) set financial and satisfaction goals for every customer.
- You (try to) make a contact or account plan for every customer before the year starts.
- You (try to) make good use of information produced by customer database technologies.
- You (try to) get marketing, sales and all other departments with customer contacts to work together in teams.

Let us see what this might mean for your company.

MEASURING AND IMPROVING THE PERFORMANCE OF EVERY CUSTOMER

By now you know that customer marketing means applying statistical process control techniques to commercial processes. The customer marketing methodology provides you with the means to measure and manage the key performance factors for every customer:

- customer value (profitability)
- customer behaviour (revenue)
- customer satisfaction (satisfaction scores).

SETTING GOALS FOR EVERY CUSTOMER

What goals do you set for your company or business unit for a planning period? Market share? Profits? Profits as a percentage of sales? Revenue? Return on investment? These are all tried and tested managerial goals. Customer marketing does not neglect them but it does recognize the inescapable fact of life that market share, profits, sales and return on investment come from only one source: customers. Thus customer marketing requires you to translate your corporate goals into *customer goals*. As a result, you will specify how many of what kinds of customers you want to:

- identify (get prospects, leads)
- acquire (make a new customer)
- keep (maintain purchasing pattern)
- upgrade (increase purchasing)

for a given planning period.

Thus you will examine all your customers (and prospects) and for each one set a goal in terms of:

- what profitability you plan to get from each customer/prospect
- what revenues you plan to get from each customer/prospect
- what satisfaction scores you plan to get from each customer/prospect.

COMMUNICATIONS: MAKING A CONTACT PLAN FOR EVERY CUSTOMER

It is one thing to set goals for customers and prospects. It is another thing entirely to 'make it happen'. The customer marketing methodology requests that for every customer or prospect with a planned goal there must be a customer contact plan which attempts to reach these goals at the least cost. The contact plans employ a mix of methods and media.

You hear and read much about 'integrated communications' these days. Usually that means some form of close coordination of a promotional campaign which combines advertising, direct marketing, sales promotion and publicity. Customer marketing calls for the planning, registration and evaluation of all contacts between the company and its customers, prospects and suspects whatever the method or media: a sales visit, a direct mail shot, a response advertisement, etc. The purpose of this integrated approach is to ensure that the most cost-effective medium and method can be employed for each customer or prospect situation. As an example, let us say you are trying to get new customers for your fax machines. You can use your sales force to call companies to find out if they have a fax; identify the decision maker; try to get a sales appointment; make the sales call; and close the deal. You will make some sales, of course. But given the high cost of a salesperson, and the limited amount of time a salesperson has (only 1400 selling hours per year), you will probably find that this mix of media and methods delivers more new customers, more sales, and at a lower cost per sale:

- *outbound telemarketing* to see if suspect companies have faxes; identify fax decision makers
- *direct mail* to the fax decision makers to generate sales leads
- *internal sales force call* to qualify the leads and make appointments for demonstrations
- *external sales force* give the demonstrations; create the customers; close the sales
- *outbound telemarketing* to non-respondents; make appointments for demonstrations.

In the case of current customers, you can substitute some routine sales visits (costing £100 each) to regular customers with programmed telephone calls ('business calls') from the sales force (costing £10 each). The customer will appreciate the service, while the cost of the customer contact is reduced by £90. If the customer places an order over the telephone – which happens more often than you may think – the cost of the sale is a mere £10!

You can use virtually every kind of media and method with customer marketing. But then you may get yourself lost in a semantic jungle trying to distinguish between 'above-the-line' and 'below-the-line' media and joining the never-ending debates about the real meaning of 'direct marketing', 'sales promotion', 'advertising', 'marketing', 'PR', 'interactive marketing'. To make life simple for yourself, categorize your selling methods and media into the matrix shown in Figure 7.1 where the four media types – personal, telephone, print and electronic – are categorized at one-to-one individual contacts versus one-to-many contacts. You can make a contact plan for each customer to reach your objective for that customer at the lowest cost. As methods and media become more personal and individual, the higher the cost per contact.

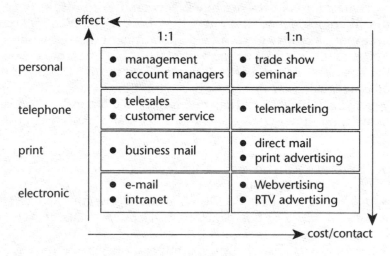

Figure 7.1 *Selling methods and media matrix*

INFORMATION: USING CUSTOMER DATABASE TECHNOLOGIES

Customer marketing requires your company to be highly customer oriented. But a customer orientation is only possible if you have a lot of information about your customers and can communicate with them personally. Let us see how a customer oriented shopkeeper uses customer information to improve his business.

Consider Mr Jones, a pharmacy proprietor in a small town. He knows a lot about his customers and prospects, having lived and worked in the town for years. He has a very sophisticated customer database system – right between his ears. When Mrs Smith walks in, Mr Jones puts down a prepared prescription and says, 'Good morning, Mrs Smith. Your monthly prescription is here waiting for you.'

'Thank you, Mr Jones,' replies Mrs Smith.

Mr Jones scans the Smith file in his customer database and retrieves some data, 'How is your husband's hip? Is it any better?' asks Mr Jones.

'Why thank you for asking', Mrs Smith responds. 'It's better, but not yet 100 per cent OK.'

Mr Jones pulls a box off the shelf and hands it to Mrs Smith. 'Why don't you try this out, Mrs Smith. We just got it in. A 16-valve, turbo-power hot water bottle. Costs just £18.71. It's supposed to work wonders. But if it doesn't, why, you just bring it right back for a refund.'

'I'll just do that,' says Mrs Smith. 'Thank you very much.'

'You're quite welcome, and have a nice day,' replies Mr Jones, putting the money in his cash register – £18.71 in extra revenue.

Here is a classic case of upgrading a regular customer through use of information about that customer. Of course, you can rely on your own memory if your customers are few and you have frequent and personal contact with them. But what if you have thousands of customers, and you do not meet them personally? The answer to this problem is your customer database. Mail order companies, publishers, credit card vendors and other sophisticated direct marketers pioneered the development of customer databases running on large, expensive mainframe computers in the 1960s and 1970s. Today, for less than £6250, you can buy a computer and database package capable of storing and managing information on tens of thousands of customers.

- *Customer identity and characteristics.* Basic data such as names, addresses, telephone numbers are a must; but also characteristics such as type of business, number of employees, etc (for business) and sex, date of birth, family size, etc (for consumers).
- *Products purchased/requests/interests.* It is also important to store information on the products and services purchased or enquired about. From this information, you can deduce interest areas – if you have not already obtained this information via surveys or other means.
- *'Total spend' factors.* Factors which determine how much the customer/prospect will spend in your category of products/ services in the coming year.

- *'Customer share' factors.* Factors which determine what percentage the customer/prospect will spend in your category with your company in the coming year.
- *Media and/or activity which influenced transaction.* You will want to know which medium – be it a sales visit or a response advertisement – led to a sale or brought you the customer in the first place.
- *A history of the customer relationship.* If you get it right, your database will contain a complete history of your relationship with each customer and prospect in your customer pyramid.

Once you have this kind of information about your customers, you can also communicate with your customers on a personal basis with two goals in mind:

1. To create a strong link with your customers, just like the old-fashioned shopkeepers used to do – even if you have 1000; 10,000; 100,000; 1,000,000 customers or more.
2. To avoid wasting marketing and sales money on suspects, prospects and customers who are unlikely to buy anything from you at that moment.

Imagine, for example, you own a clothing store and you have thousands of customers registered in your database. An analysis reveals that there are two types of women who buy baby clothes: type A women aged 59–99; and type B women aged 19–39. You use your brilliant mind to determine that type A women are probably grandmothers or aunts; type B women are probably mothers. Around 1 December you send a high-quality mailing featuring expensive and exclusive children's clothes to the type A women, with a signed, 'personal' letter which comments that they have bought children's clothes in the past, and suggests the offered collection as gift ideas. 'Thank you for thinking of me', say the type A women, reaching for their chequebooks while heading out the door to visit your store.

After the Christmas rush, you see what children's clothes are left over. These items you feature in an inexpensive mailing sent to type B women as a post-Christmas sale of fine clothes at reduced prices. 'Thank you for thinking of me', say the type B women, reaching for their chequebooks, smiling secretly at the fact that they can purchase the same items as their mothers-in-law a few weeks before but at a 30 per cent discount!

Customer marketing makes people happy. Especially those who practise it. The same principles apply, whether you are selling bulldozers or baby clothes but it will only work if you have collected information about your customers and prospects in your customer database and can manage and manipulate the information efficiently. Thus a good system supports all the phases of the customer marketing process: registration, analysis, planning and realization (Figure 7.2).

registration
- customer value
- customer loyalty
- customer satisfaction
- customer orientation

realization
- with customers
- about customers

analysis
- ROI
- customer lifetime
- customer scores

planning
- customer goals
- product offers
- media/methods

Figure 7.2 *Customer marketing supported by a customer information system*

ORGANIZATION: INSTALLING CUSTOMER TEAMS

'Nobody knows who I am!'; 'I keep getting transferred from one department to another!'; 'Why don't they communicate with each other?' These often-heard customer complaints, result from the existence of 'stand alone' departments (see Figure 7.3); where departments such as finance, marketing, production, service, sales and logistics all act independently of each other in their dealings with customers.

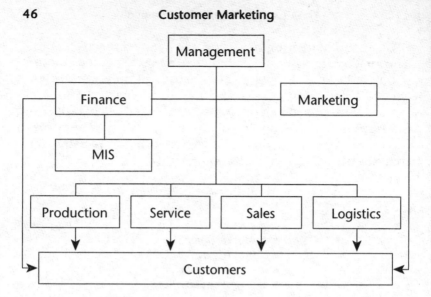

Figure 7.3 *'Standalone' departments*

Some companies try to solve this problem by 'putting the customer on top' (see Figure 7.4) but it does not make any difference because the 'stand alone' departments deal with the customer from their own narrow perspective, leading to customer confusion and anger. At some companies the following scenario is not unusual.

'Buy this product,' suggests Sales. And the customer agreed.

'What? You bought this machine? I could have kept the old one going for another year,' cries Service.

'It'll take three months to make,' says Production.

'What order, for what machine?' asks Logistics.

'We love you, we love you!' is the message of the brochure sent by Marketing.

'Pay or Die!' is the message of the letter sent by Accounts with the invoice which arrives in the same batch of mail as Marketing's love letter.

The answer to this cluster of problems is to form 'customer teams'. The customer team is a powerful and fundamental customer marketing concept. The primary customer team consists of people who have or are responsible for contacts with a specific group of customers, often represented in a customer pyramid. In business-to-business situations, the roster of a customer team often looks like the following.

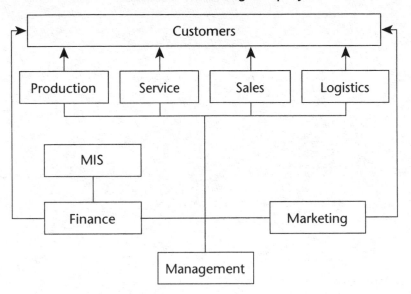

Figure 7.4 *Putting the customer 'on top'*

- The *account manager* or field salesperson assigned to the customer.
- The *telesales* person who is 'paired' to the account manager or assigned to the customer.
- The *service representative* whose route or territory includes the customer.
- A *marketing person*, who may have responsibility for marketing communications or a product manager who represents the marketing department in the team.

In some instances, the customer team can be enriched with representatives from other departments such as finance, production, logistics, etc (Figure 7.5).

We will see later how customer teams work in practice. But a few key customer team principles should be explained now.

- A customer manager is appointed for each customer depending on the situation. For instance, the account manager is manager of customer X; telesales is manager of customer Y; marketing is manager of suspect Z. The customer manager is responsible for detecting problems and buying signals while ensuring that the proper person takes the proper action to achieve the goal. (Important: the customer does not know

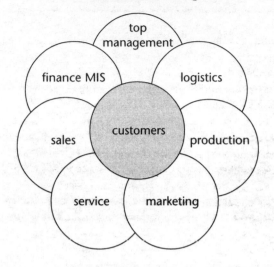

Figure 7.5 *The customer team*

who is the customer manager, since this function can change
quickly depending on the situation.)

- The customer team is responsible for setting goals for each
  customer in their customer pyramid. For instance, the team
  may plan that customer X will migrate from 'small' to 'top'
  status in the customer pyramid, and customer Y, a 'small'
  customer, will remain a 'small' customer.
- The customer team concurs on the contact plan for each
  customer in their customer pyramid. For instance, customer
  X should be visited six times by the account manager next
  year, and customer Y should only be called four times by
  telesales; suspect Z should be invited to the trade show.

8

Is Customer Marketing Right for Your Company?

By now you should have a good idea about what the customer marketing methodology is and how your company may have to adapt and change if you decide to go ahead and implement it. In our experience, implementing any kind of change in an organization can lead to some disruption and resistance: the same holds true for customer marketing. Managers who implement customer marketing are confronted with protests like these:

'We tried something like this five years ago and it didn't work.'
'We're doing OK, why should we do it differently?'
'*My* customers won't like it.'
'Marketing and sales are intuitive, you can't measure everything.'

Will the investment in time and money be worth while? Here is a quick test to help you decide. Below are four main statements about activities of companies which have implemented customer marketing. For each main statement you can evaluate your own situation by determining the degree to which:

- the activity applies to your company
- improvement in this area would help you to reach your business goals.

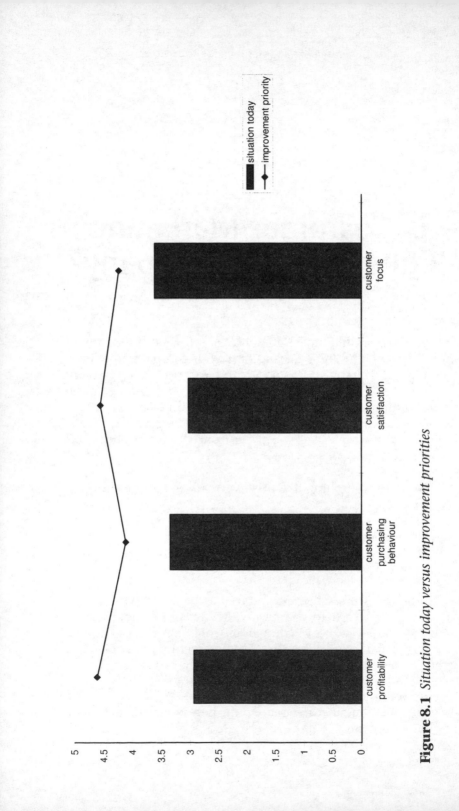

Figure 8.1 *Situation today versus improvement priorities*

Scoring is as follows:

5 = this statement is absolutely true
4 = this statement is more or less true
3 = this statement is equally true and false
2 = this statement is more or less false
1 = this statement is absolutely false

Try it out!

We work at measuring and improving the
profitability of every customer.

a. This is the situation at our company today   1 2 3 4 5
b. Improvement in this area would help us
    achieve our business goals   1 2 3 4 5

We work at measuring and improving the
purchasing behaviour of every customer.

a. This is the situation at our company today   1 2 3 4 5
b. Improvement in this area would help us
    achieve our business goals   1 2 3 4 5

We work at measuring and improving the
satisfaction of every customer.

a. This is the situation at our company today   1 2 3 4 5
b. Improvement in this area would help us
    achieve our business goals   1 2 3 4 5

We work at measuring and improving the
customer focus of our company's organization,
communications and information.

a. This is the situation at our company today   1 2 3 4 5
b. Improvement in this area would help us
    achieve our business goals   1 2 3 4 5

Check out your scores. Are there substantial gaps between the
situation today and your improvement priorities? (See Figure
8.1.)
    If so, then you will want to move on to Part II.

Part II

How to Make Customer Marketing Work in Your Company

9

The Process in Detail

In Part I of this book we described and visualized customer marketing as a structured business methodology which uses process control techniques to meet profitability targets by setting and achieving goals for customer performance and customer focus.

The customer performance factors are:

- customer value
- customer behaviour
- customer satisfaction.

The customer focus factors are:

- organization
- communications
- information.

Now is the time to look at the customer marketing process in detail. In the following chapters we will describe the following four phases of the customer marketing methodology, phase by phase and step by step (see Figure 9.1).

PHASE I: CUSTOMER MARKETING REGISTRATION

Register customer value

1. Define a customer
2. Register number of customers

Figure 9.1 *The customer marketing methodology*

3. Register operational profit
4. Register marketing and sales costs
5. Register average profit per customer
6. Register average return on investment on marketing and sales

Register customer behaviour

1. Define customer behaviour variable for your customer pyramid
2. Register historical customer behaviour
3. Rank customers by behaviour variable
4. Create a customer pyramid
5. Define and register total spend factors
6. Define and register customer share factors

Register customer satisfaction

1. Determine value propositions (product, service, 'extras')
2. Register customer scores of importance of and satisfaction with value propositions
3. Register customer loyalty indicators

Register customer focus

1. Audit customer focus – organization (management and employees)
2. Audit customer focus – communications (contact logistics, methods/media)
3. Audit customer focus – information (customer data and system)

PHASE II: CUSTOMER MARKETING ANALYSIS

Analyse customer value

1. Allocate margins and costs to individual customers and/or pyramid segments
2. Analyse profit and contribution per customer and/or pyramid segments
3. Analyse ROI on marketing and sales per customer and/or pyramid segments

Analyse customer behaviour

1. Create and analyse a historical migration matrix
2. Analyse total spend factors
3. Analyse customer share factors
4. Perform 'what-if?' scenarios with a planning matrix

Analyse customer satisfaction

1. Analyse importance versus satisfaction to identify improvement areas
2. Analyse loyalty indicators
3. Identify unhappy customers
4. Select departments and people to join the improvement groups

Analyse customer focus

1. Analyse gaps: situation versus priorities
2. Identify priorities for improvement in your organization, communications and information
3. Install customer focus improvement groups for organization, communications and information

PHASE III: CUSTOMER MARKETING PLANNING

Plan customer value

1. Set top-down corporate targets: revenues, profits, market share, etc
2. Set top-down budgets for
   - methods and media
   - customer benefits
   - customer satisfaction programmes

Planning customer behaviour

1. Statistical scoring per customer/prospect
2. Contact scoring per customer/prospect
3. Customer team sets targets and goal for each customer/prospect
4. Set contact norms per migration matrix cell
5. Calculate 'default mode' contact plans
6. Customer team consensus on contact plans

Plan customer satisfaction

1. Set top-down customer satisfaction targets
2. Improvement teams propose satisfaction improvement programme plans for all customers
3. Customer teams make satisfaction plans and goals for unhappy customers

Plan customer focus

1. Set top-down customer focus targets
2. Improvement groups make plans to resolve problems

PHASE IV: CUSTOMER MARKETING REALIZATION

Realization of customer value plans

1. Progress checks for profit targets
2. Monitor expenses
3. Adjust/fine-tune as required

Realization of customer behaviour plans

1. Progress check behaviour targets
2. Progress check contact targets
3. Adjust/fine-tune as required

Realization of customer satisfaction plans

1. Progress check unhappy customers
2. Progress check departmental actions
3. Adjust/fine-tune as required

Realization of customer focus plans

1. Progress check customer focus targets
2. Progress check improvement plans
3. Adjust/fine-tune as required

RE-REGISTRATION: CLOSING THE CUSTOMER MARKETING LOOP

- Re-register customer focus
- Re-register customer satisfaction
- Re-register customer behaviour
- Re-register customer value

INTRODUCING 'INTERTECH'

To explain and illustrate customer marketing implementation we will follow the progress of 'InterTech'. InterTech is a notional company operation in the notional country of Ruritania; but the InterTech patterns of customer values, behaviour and satisfaction have been drawn from numerous actual companies which we have examined closely in the past six years. The status of customer focus inside InterTech – the organization, communications and information – is representative of companies we have studied.

InterTech is a wholesaler of electronic components. As such, it is a business-to-business company with an external sales force. We have selected a business-to-business case simply because there are more business-to-business companies than business-to-consumer companies. (Excluding, perhaps, retail stores. Nonetheless, customer marketing is used with success by retailers, makers of fast moving consumer goods, financial services suppliers – even lawyers and consultants.)

InterTech is fairly small, with annual revenues of R$2 million (the Ruritanian dollar is similar to an ECU or about US$1). But if you are working in a larger company, you might recognize InterTech as having many characteristics of an autonomous business unit or branch office. Last – but certainly not least – the InterTech customers are manufacturers or assemblers of consumer products (washing machines) and industrial machinery.

How did customer marketing work at InterTech? What can you learn from their experiences? Let us find out, beginning with some preliminary steps to take before you enter Phase I.

ORGANIZING THE IMPLEMENTATION EFFORT

Make your management team the customer marketing steering committee

Customer marketing needs management commitment to make it work; and the methodology involves the whole company or business unit. Thus it makes sense to put the implementation 'in the line' by avoiding the creation of a steering committee or some similar body to oversee the implementation process. Simply add 'customer marketing progress report' to the fixed agenda points of the management team meeting. The primary function of the management team as steering committee is to make top-down decisions about goals and budgets which will stimulate bottom-up responses ending, normally, in consensus on company goals and budgets, resolve cross-departmental disputes, etc.

Install a customer marketing project group

The customer marketing project group is charged with timely and effective implementation of the methodology and reports to the management team/steering committee. You should appoint a customer marketing project group with representatives from marketing, field sales, telesales, service, IT and other groups with heavy customer contact.

A minimum customer marketing project group should consist of a project manager – a 'make-it-happen' person with respect and authority, who may also be a member of the management team – and a minimum of three other people, each with knowledge of and responsibility for the areas of customer information, customer organization and customer communications, since they may be heading up improvement groups in these areas charged with improving customer satisfaction and customer focus.

Install customer teams

Customer teams, as described in Part I of this book, will play an important part in the introduction and execution of the customer marketing methodology. Since the customer team cuts across department boundaries it fosters cooperation among the members who are bound together to meet a common objective: get them in, move them up and keep them in!

Customers are also happy with customer teams because customers tend to get more personal attention, and their contacts within your company appear to be more responsive because of the improved information flow among the team members. Normally, each customer team works with a specific set of customers in a region, and works with a customer pyramid representing the customers in that region.

The end result is a simple structure set up to start improving your customer performance and customer focus through the implementation of customer marketing (Figure 9.2). Now let us get down to the real work!

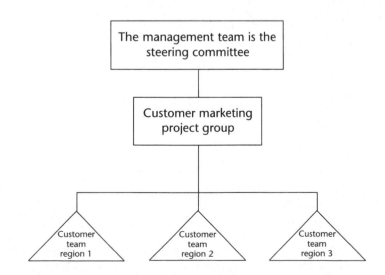

Figure 9.2 *Customer marketing implementation: getting started*

10

Phase I: Customer Marketing Registration

This phase of customer marketing involves the collection and storage of data and information on your customer performance. If you are doing this for the first time, you will probably discover that much of the information you need is stored in various formats at different locations all over the company, such as:

- the accounts department
- service contracts and records
- the logistics department and mail room
- in the diaries – and heads – of the sales force

Do not despair – it becomes easier the second time around. We will also help you to decide which information you *need to know* versus information which is nice to know so that you can focus on the priorities.

REGISTER CUSTOMER VALUE

Most of the information related to customer value – or profit per customer – can be found in the accounts department and financial reports. What you do with this information is 'customer-based accounting' or CBA. (CBA is a customer-based version of 'activity-based costing', or ABC!) Controllers, administrators and other financial people – not often known to be champions of marketing and sales spending – often become enthusiastic about CBA. If so, they will be of invaluable assistance in helping you to analyse, plan and budget your marketing and sales activities.

1. Define a customer

It is essential, of course, to define your customers as discussed in Chapter 3 on customer pyramids. At InterTech, *active customers* were defined as companies or decision-making units within a company authorized to write a purchase order which purchased goods and services within the last 12 months. *Inactive customers* had purchased goods and services more than 12 months before.

2. Register number of customers

Amazingly enough, many companies cannot determine how many customers they have. Part of the problem comes from the definition – what or who is our customer? Another road-block is that there is no way to register customers, as in retail scores. Hence the rise of 'customer cards'.

For most business-to-business companies which bill clients, you can count up the number of customers who received invoices last year and this is the number of customers, but beware: perhaps like you, InterTech has some large companies as customers. InterTech invoices go to different departments with different identifying numbers, thus giving the impression of more customers than is the case. But some of these departments actually qualify as different customers according to InterTech's definition of a customer. An 'eyeball' check of your customer list is always necessary. In the end, InterTech counted 450 active customers.

3. Register operational profit

Operational profit is sometimes called 'EBDIT' or earnings before depreciation, interest and taxes. This number is a reflection of company performance based on transactions with customers. InterTech operational profits were R$91,499 as shown in Table 10.1.

4. Register marketing and sales costs

This step is necessary because marketing and sales costs have the same impact on the profitability of a customer as revenue and margin per customer. What are marketing and sales costs? You may find it useful to use the following three cost clusters.

- *Sales costs* are those commercial costs incurred to influence the buying behaviour of individual customers. Thus the

Table 10.1 *InterTech operational results*

	R$	%
Revenues	2,026,983	100
Direct costs	1,183,484	58
Margin %	42%	
Margin	843,499	42
General sales and administrative costs (GSA)	752,000	37
Operational profit	91,499	5

salaries and expenses of the field sales force, telesales people and (sometimes) service people are considered to be sales costs.

- *Marketing costs* are those commercial costs spent on activities to influence the buying behaviour of customer groups, rather than individual customers: direct mail, advertising, publicity, telemarketing campaigns, etc.
- *Marketing and sales overheads* are indirect costs of the marketing and sales department: management costs and fees, office space, automation and other overheads absorbed by marketing and sales.

And when you deduct sales costs, marketing costs and marketing and sales overheads from the general sales and administrative costs, the remainder is pure overheads. In Table 10.2 you see the marketing, sales and overhead costs identified at InterTech.

5. Register average profit per customer
6. Register average return on investment on marketing and sales

The *average turnover and profit per customer* is calculated by dividing revenue and profit by number of (active) customers. The *average Return on Investment (ROI) for marketing and sales* is calculated by dividing profit by all marketing and sales costs. The primary function of this ROI calculation is to provide a baseline measurement against which to judge improvements. InterTech had 450 active customers last year, so the revenue per customer was R$4,504 and profit per customer R$203 (Table 10.3).

This financial view is often quite surprising for management. Most managers underestimate actual marketing and sales costs

Table 10.2 *Marketing, sales and overhead costs at InterTech*

Sales costs	R$
Field sales	158,000
Internal sales	100,000
Customer service	25,000
Travel, representation	19,000
Total sales costs	302,000
Marketing costs	
Advertising	4,000
Mailings	3,000
Telemarketing	2,000
Exhibition	10,000
Representation	3,000
PR publicity	2,000
Customer benefits	1,000
Total marketing costs	25,000
M&S overheads	
Sales management	25,000
Marketing management	25,000
Automation	6,000
Office	4,000
Miscellaneous	10,000
Total M&S overheads	70,000
General overheads	
Office	127,500
General costs	170,000
Depreciation	43,000
Interest	14,500
Total overheads	355,000

Table 10.3 *InterTech customer value and ROI*

	R$	%
Revenues	2,026,983	100
Direct costs	1,183,484	58
Margin %	42%	
Margin	843,499	42
General overheads	355,000	18
Profit before M&S	488,499	24
Marketing & sales		
Sales costs	302,000	15
Marketing costs	25,000	1
M&S overheads	70,000	3
Total M&S costs	397,000	20
Operational profit	91,499	5
Customers	450	
Revenue per customer	4,504	
Profit per customer	203	
ROI on M&S	23%	

since a large portion may be hidden in overheads. Few managers have ever considered figuring out the ROI on marketing and sales spend. These numbers, while interesting, will be more useful when we drill down to the customer level later on.

REGISTER CUSTOMER BEHAVIOUR

1. Define customer behaviour variable for your customer pyramid

Customer pyramids reflect customer behaviour. You want to choose the variable which is easy to register and analyse, of course. More importantly, it should be a variable that you can influence by your marketing and sales efforts. More often than not, the single most important customer behaviour item is purchasing: how much did each customer spend with us last year? And the year before that? InterTech chose customer revenue as the variable for building the customer pyramid.

2. Register historical customer behaviour

These numbers are hard to come by in a retail or fast mover situation where transactions per customer are not registered. You have to work with research data or tests in several stores and then extrapolate results. Getting sales per customer data in business-to-business situations is not always easy either, even if invoices are sent out for each purchase. Why? Because accounting records may show 12 different customer numbers at one company. This may be because there is only one customer at that company, but the company named is typed in 12 different ways. Or it may be that there are 12 different business units at the company, each of which is authorized to purchase your products and services; thus 12 different customers. Usually it is a combination of the two situations. And so there is no substitute for getting a list of customers and their purchases over the year from accounts, loading it into Excel or Lotus 1-2-3 and consolidating the data based on knowledge held in the heads of sales, service and administrative people who know the customer.

3. Rank customers by behaviour variable

Once you have the customer behaviour data in a spreadsheet, you can then rank your customers from top to bottom. The result is a 'customer sort' – a list of customers for the past year with their sales revenues over a given period. In InterTech's case, the variable is sales revenue. If possible, list revenues for two consecutive years so you can track customer migration.

4. Create a customer pyramid

Building the customer pyramid is not such a problem when you have a 'customer sort'. The key is to decide how you will segment your customers, and set the 'borders' of the pyramid accordingly. (Inactive customers are on the books but without any sales revenues. The number of prospects and suspects you have to find out from the sales and marketing managers.)

InterTech chose the standard pyramid model. The customer sort indicated that the customers are segmented by the standard types: top (1 per cent); Big (4 per cent); medium (15 per cent) and small (80 per cent). InterTech discovered that its 450 customers consist of four 'tops', 18 'big', 68 'medium' and 360 'small'. (See Figure 3.3 on p 12.)

At this stage is it most useful to build a customer pyramid with this basic customer behaviour information. It is usually an eye-opener for managers who discover how few customers keep the company afloat, and for sceptics who think that the company is immune from the Pareto principle.

As we go deeper into various aspects of customer marketing we will want to look at how it works at the level of the individual customer. We will therefore select a number of InterTech customers from each level of the pyramid, which we will call the 'customer selection'. A customer selection is also quite useful as a tool when implementing customer marketing: the customer teams can practise with a limited number of customers before rolling out to all customers. The InterTech customer selection is given in Table 10.4 and shows the purchasing behaviour of each customer last year per product type, and the pyramid position last year.

Table 10.4 *InterTech customer behaviour at the customer level*

Customer name	Last year revenue	Last year pyramid	Products purchased last year R$		
			A category	B category	C category
Struckman	296,337	Top	8,890	270,200	17,247
Boards Unlimited	143,945	Top	97,883	42,838	3,224
Silicon Sync	42,365	Big	35,163	4,105	3,097
Green Machine	31,010	Big	10,543	5,321	15,145
SpeedServ	13,659	Medium	11,200	910	1,549
Main	13,026	Medium	7,164	1,465	4,396
Sentinel Service	12,604	Medium	1,765	7,154	3,685
Colby Corp.	4,791	Small	2,827	1,198	766
Bates Milling	1,717	Small	1,717	0	0
Montpelier SA	680	Small	537	1	141
de Vries Inc.	97	Small	56	9	32
Bristol	0	Inactive	0	0	0
Wilkes Corp	0	Inactive	0	0	0
Jones & Long	0	Prospect	0	0	0
British Techno	0	Prospect	0	0	0
Cellular Tel	0	Prospect	0	0	0
Bowdoin Bros.	0	Prospect	0	0	0

5. Define and register total spend factors

It is essential to know or estimate your customers' current purchasing behaviour in your category of product and services, ie the total spend. Factors to estimate customer total spend next year may vary from industry to industry. But last year's total spend – how much the customer spent last year in your category – is a key indicator to what they will spend next year. Other factors which will determine total buying potential may be size of company or family composition; age of capital equipment which is generally replaced after three years; spending plans and budgets, etc.

In some industries, information to determine total spend is easy to get. For instance vehicle registrations are public, and the size and composition of a company's fleet of vehicles and trucks is public information. Since most fleet owners replace vehicles after three years, you only have to divide the fleet size by three to determine how many vehicles they are likely to buy next year.

In other cases, total spend may not be difficult to estimate if you collect only one or two bits of information. For example, if you know the number and ages of people in a family, you can figure out fairly accurately the amount of money that family will spend each year on groceries and clothing. There is a wealth of publicly available information about businesses which can help you determine your customer share: industry codes, size of company expressed in employees or revenues; computer equipment installed on the premises, etc.

Sometimes the information you need to determine buying potential is simply not available. So how can you get it? Simply ask your customers and prospects! If you ask them properly – and give them an incentive to respond – people will volunteer plenty of information. Several years ago in England we wanted to know about the photocopying behaviour of larger companies, so we asked the person in charge of copiers to tell us:

● How may copies per month are produced in your company?
● How many copying machines were installed in your company?
● What is the brand and model number of your machines?
● When is the expiration date of the rental contract for each machine?

How many companies supplied this information? No less than 70 per cent! Why did they supply this information? Because the respondent was promised an analysis of copying patterns in his industry against which he could evaluate his own situation. (Plus an evening at a health club and the chance to win a weekend vacation...)

Table 10.5 shows the customer potential factors registered for the customers in the InterTech customer sort.

- The total spend of the customer last year.
- The size of a customer, coded by total turnover.
- The industry of a customer, listed by the first number of the SIC code.

Table 10.5 *InterTech total spend factors*

Customer name	Last year total spend	Last year total pyramid	Customer size code	Customer SIC code
Struckman	592,700	Top	5	9
Boards Unlimited	202,700	Top	5	9
Silicon Sync	529,600	Top	4	8
Green Machine	34,800	Big	2	8
SpeedServ	151,800	Top	4	7
Main	13,000	Medium	1	6
Sentinel Service	18,300	Big	1	8
Colby Corp.	110,000	Top	2	5
Bates Milling	18,900	Big	2	8
Montpelier SA	7,000	Medium	2	7
de Vries Inc.	4,600	Small	1	5
Bristol	58,000	Top	4	8
Wilkes Corp	45,000	Big	3	6
Jones & Long	158,000	Top	5	9
British Techno	43,000	Big	5	9
Cellular Tel	12,000	Medium	2	8
Bowdoin Bros.	3,900	Small	4	6

6. Define and register customer share factors

Share of customer is the amount of purchasing a customer does with you as a percentage of their total spend in your business category. For example, you sell £100,000 in a year to both customer A and customer B. Customer A's total spend that year was £1,000,000; for customer B it was £200,000. Thus your share of customer for customer A is 10 per cent and for customer B it is 50 per cent. What factors determine the share you get from your customers? InterTech determined that these factors were important for determining potential 'share of customer' (see also Table 10.6).

- The share of customer achieved last year.
- The degree of customer satisfaction (see the next section on this topic).
- The primary competitor fighting against InterTech for the business.
- The sales region (and sales person) which serves the customer.

REGISTER CUSTOMER SATISFACTION

This phase of customer marketing involves the collection and storage of data and information on the satisfaction of your customers. You can carry out a customer satisfaction survey through face-to-face interviews, telephone calls or by written questionnaires; and you can decide to do it yourself or have it done by an external research company. It is a question of calculating the time and costs required to make the measurement of every customer. Some managers say to us, 'What? A customer satisfaction survey for every customer? It will cost too much money! We will do a small sample and we will know what our customers think about us and what we have to improve.' If you are selling fast moving consumer goods, measuring satisfaction level of all customers buying low margin products is not practical.

The fact remains that satisfaction is one of the most important facts you will ever need to know about each individual customer: because the satisfaction level of a customer largely determines if the customer will fade away, keep buying, or perhaps recruit more customers for you. The satisfaction level will largely determine what plans and activities you will carry out for that customer, and how you will communicate.

Table 10.6 *InterTech share of customer factors*

Customer name	Last year total spend	Last year revenue	Last year share of customer (%)	Customer satisfaction	Main competition	Sales region
Struckman	592,700	296,337	50	4.2	Delta	Merlin
Boards Unlimited	202,700	143,945	71	3.7	Data B	Alice
Silicon Sync	529,600	42,365	8	2.2	Delta	Alice
Green Machine	34,800	31,010	89	3.3	Smit	Merlin
SpeedServ	151,800	13,659	9	3.8	Delta	Merlin
Main	13,000	13,026	100	2.7	Sole Supp	Alice
Sentinel Service	18,300	12,604	69	3.7	Delta	Merlin
Colby Corp.	110,000	4,791	4	3.5	Delta	Alice
Bates Milling	18,900	1,717	25	3.0	Smit	Alice
Montpelier SA	7,000	680	67	3.2	Data B	Merlin
de Vries Inc.	4,600	97	101	4.0	Sole Supp	Alice
Bristol	58,000	0			Smit	Merlin
Wilkes Corp	45,000	0			Delta	Alice
Jones & Long	158,000	0			Smit	Merlin
British Techno	43,000	0			Smit	Alice
Cellular Tel	12,000	0			Delta	Alice
Bowdoin Bros.	3,900	0			Data B	Merlin

For many companies the cost of acquiring the information – about £6 per customer via a telephone survey – is a fraction of the cost of preparing the 12 monthly invoices they send to the customer each year. Yet the satisfaction level of the customer will, to a great extent, determine how long they will be sending out invoices to those customers! In short, customer satisfaction measurement is a critical customer marketing stop. You will use the information gained to make improvements in the satisfaction level on the individual customer level as well as for all customers. To start you need to think about what questions to ask using the concept of 'value propositions'.

1. Determine value propositions (product, service, 'extras')

Customer satisfaction scores are important but just as important is the need to measure the importance customers place on each of your 'value propositions'.

Figure 10.1 shows the three main categories of 'value propositions'.

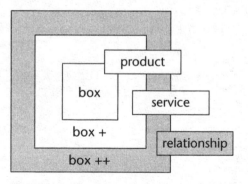

Figure 10.1 *Identifying 'value propositions'*

● The 'box' value propositions are the basic products (or services) you deliver to your customers, ie suits, temporary help workers or fuel for vehicles.
● The 'box +' value propositions are the service aspects which accompany your basic product, such as fixing the cuffs of the suit, handling the social security payments of the temporary help and wiping your windows when you fill up the petrol tank.

- The 'box ++' value propositions are those relationship factors which make you very comfortable, happy and ready to buy again, such as giving you a free neck tie with your suit, having the temporary secretary bring you a bunch of flowers on her first day and the attendant knowing your name when you fill up at the petrol pump.

The InterTech managers and staff got together in a workshop session and came up with the following list of value propositions.

- Quality of products:
    1. widgets
    2. plunkets
    3. Johnson Bars
    4. Whamos
- Service quality:
    5. maintenance contract
    6. consulting services
- Relationship quality:
    7. range of services
    8. price level
    9. geographical location
    10. problem-solving ability
    11. offer 'tailor made' services to your company
    12. offer useful ideas and suggestions (proactive)
    13. availability by phone in general
    14. written correspondence is customer-friendly
    15. handling complaints
    16. international company with large R&D department
    17. expertise of your contact person
    18. availability of your contact person
    19. customer orientation of your contact person
    20. keeping appointments.

2. Register customer scores of importance of and satisfaction with value propositions

A customer marketing satisfaction survey does not measure satisfaction alone but also shows discrepancies or 'gaps' between the importance of a value proposition and satisfaction. Thus for each value proposition you ask two questions: how *important* is this aspect for you: 5 = highly important; 4 = important;

3 = neutral; 2 = not important; 1 = irrelevant. Then for that value proposition you ask: how *satisfied* are you with this aspect: 5 = highly satisfied; 4 = satisfied; 3 = neutral; 2 = unsatisfied; 1 = highly unsatisfied. For example, you may score '4.5' for satisfaction on your corporate brochures and '4.5' for speed of delivery. But if customers score the value or importance of your brochures as '3.4' and '4.8' for speed of delivery, you really must focus on fixing speed of delivery... and quickly!

3. Register customer loyalty indicators

Also important to ask are questions which indicate the loyalty of a customer. The following are three primary loyalty indicators and scoring methods.

- Does the customer consider you the preferred supplier?
  5 = sole supplier; 4 = preferred supplier; 3 = equal opportunity; 2 = low preference; 1 = undesired
- Is the customer planning to buy from you next year?
  5 = definitely; 4 = probably; 3 = neutral; 2 = probably not; 1 = definitely not
- Would the customer recommend you to colleagues, friends and family?
  5 = definitely; 4 = probably; 3 = neutral; 2 = probably not; 1 = definitely not

InterTech carried out a telephone survey to all customers. The telephone contact with the customer was also used to fill in missing data on the 'total spend' and 'customer share' factors. Figures 10.2 and 10.3 summarize the InterTech results.

REGISTER CUSTOMER FOCUS

How can you measure and analyse the customer focus of your company? Of course the results of the customer satisfaction survey will give you some input. But to get a very clear view on the customer focus of your company you have to ask the experts. By this we mean the men and women on the work floor who are dealing with customers every day, know their complaints, know how it can be done better.

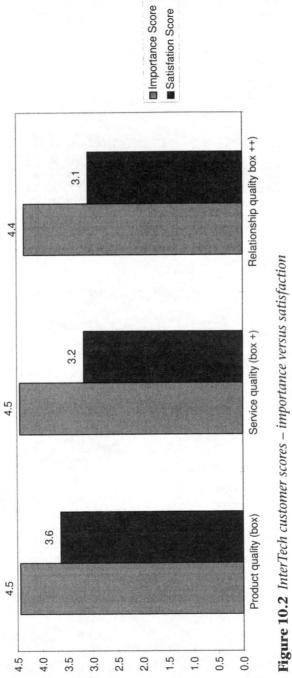

Figure 10.2 *InterTech customer scores – importance versus satisfaction*

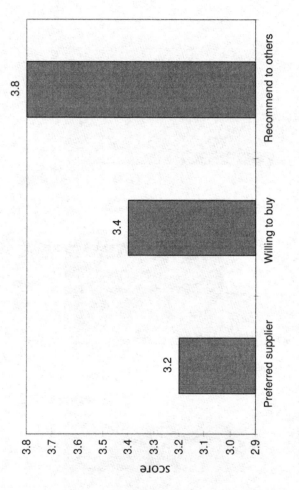

Figure 10.3 *InterTech customer loyalty indicator scores*

1. Audit customer focus – organization (management and employees)
2. Audit customer focus – communications (contact logistics, methods/media)
3. Audit customer focus – information (customer data and system)

You can use this simple self-assessment tool which registers two things.

● How you and your 'experts' evaluate the current situation for each item.
● The degree to which they evaluate that this item is important to the company.

You can score each of the customer focus statements as follows:

5 = I agree totally with this statement
4 = I agree somewhat with this statement
3 = I am neutral about this statement
2 = I disagree somewhat with this statement
1 = I disagree totally with this statement

Organization – management

1. Management is committed to improving the customer focus of our company.

    a. This is the situation at our company today   1 2 3 4 5
    b. Improvement in this area would help us
       achieve our business goals   1 2 3 4 5

2. Management sets an example for customer focus by their own actions.

    a. This is the situation at our company today   1 2 3 4 5
    b. Improvement in this area would help us
       achieve our business goals   1 2 3 4 5

3. Management provides a sufficient budget (especially time) to improve customer focus.

    a. This is the situation at our company today   1 2 3 4 5
    b. Improvement in this area would help us
       achieve our business goals   1 2 3 4 5

Organization – employees

4. Our employees have sufficient know-how and experience to deal with customers properly.

    a. This is the situation at our company today   1 2 3 4 5
    b. Improvement in this area would help us
       achieve our business goals   1 2 3 4 5

5. The customer's needs are central in the thoughts and actions of our employees.

    a. This is the situation at our company today   1 2 3 4 5
    b. Improvement in this area would help us
       achieve our business goals   1 2 3 4 5

6. Departments with customer contact work together with a team spirit.

    a. This is the situation at our company today   1 2 3 4 5
    b. Improvement in this area would help us
       achieve our business goals   1 2 3 4 5

Communication – methods, media, messages

7. We use the most effective methods and media to accomplish goals at the lowest cost.

    a. This is the situation at our company today   1 2 3 4 5
    b. Improvement in this area would help us
       achieve our business goals   1 2 3 4 5

8. Our communications with customers demonstrate that we know them and their needs.

    a. This is the situation at our company today   1 2 3 4 5
    b. Improvement in this area would help us
       achieve our business goals   1 2 3 4 5

9. Our customer communications stress the benefits of our products and services rather than describing their features.

    a. This is the situation at our company today   1 2 3 4 5
    b. Improvement in this area would help us
       achieve our business goals   1 2 3 4 5

Communication – contact logistics

10. A contact and communication plan is made
    for every customer.

    a. This is the situation at our company today   1 2 3 4 5

    b. Improvement in this area would help us
    achieve our business goals   1 2 3 4 5

11. The execution of customer contacts is
    registered in procedures and diaries.

    a. This is the situation at our company today   1 2 3 4 5

    b. Improvement in this area would help us
    achieve our business goals   1 2 3 4 5

12. Non-commercial communications
    (correspondence, invoices, etc) is 'customer-
    friendly'.

    a. This is the situation at our company today   1 2 3 4 5

    b. Improvement in this area would help us
    achieve our business goals   1 2 3 4 5

Information – data on customers

13. We have information which is useful to
    determine customer potential and to
    communicate with the right customer,
    about the right product, at the right time.

    a. This is the situation at our company today   1 2 3 4 5

    b. Improvement in this area would help us
    achieve our business goals   1 2 3 4 5

14. Our customer information is complete.

    a. This is the situation at our company today   1 2 3 4 5

    b. Improvement in this area would help us
    achieve our business goals   1 2 3 4 5

15. Our customer information is up to date.

    a. This is the situation at our company today   1 2 3 4 5

    b. Improvement in this area would help us
    achieve our business goals   1 2 3 4 5

Table 10.7 *Registration of customer focus scores*

Domain	Number	Item	Situation	Priority	'Gap'
Org–mgt	1	Management is committed	3.5	4.1	0.6
Org–mgt	2	Management sets an example	3.3	3.9	0.6
Org–mgt	3	Management allocates (time) budget	2.6	3.8	1.2
Org–staff	4	Know-how and experience	2.1	4.5	2.4
Org–staff	5	Customer focus attitude	2.1	4.4	2.3
Org–staff	6	People work in teams	1.8	3.8	2.0
Organization			2.6	4.1	1.5
Comms/MMM	7	Best method at lowest cost	2.2	4.1	1.9
Comms/MMM	8	Personalized communication	3.1	4.2	1.1
Comms/MMM	9	Benefit oriented	3.2	3.7	0.5
Comms–cont log	10	Contact plan for every customer	2.3	4.5	2.2
Comms–cont log	11	Procedures for contacts	2.3	4.2	1.9
Comms–cont log	12	Customer-friendly communications	2.8	3.7	0.9
Communications			2.7	4.1	1.4
Info–cus info	13	Information is relevant	2.4	4.2	1.8
Info–cus info	14	Information is complete	2.1	4.4	2.3
Info–cus info	15	Information is up to date	1.9	4.3	2.4
Info–systems	16	System is effective	2.2	4.1	1.9
Info–systems	17	System is flexible	1.6	4.3	2.7
Info–systems	18	System is accessible	1.8	4.5	2.7
Information			2.0	4.3	2.3
Totals			2.4	4.2	1.7

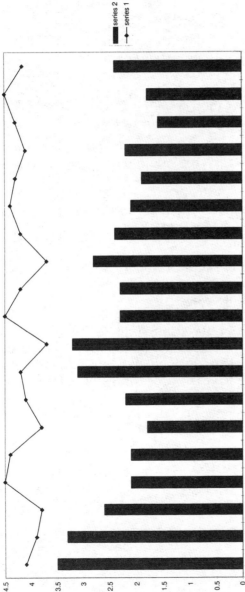

Figure 10.4 *InterTech customer focus gaps chart*

Information – customer information system

16. Our customer information system makes it easy
to analyse customers and communicate with them
via mail, telephone and face-to-face.

    a. This is the situation at our company today   1 2 3 4 5
    b. Improvement in this area would help us
       achieve our business goals   1 2 3 4 5

17. Our customer information system is flexible
(easy to make changes to meet our needs).

    a. This is the situation at our company today   1 2 3 4 5
    b. Improvement in this area would help us
       achieve our business goals   1 2 3 4 5

18. Our customer information system can make
available information about customers to
anyone who needs it.

    a. This is the situation at our company today   1 2 3 4 5
    b. Improvement in this area would help us
       achieve our business goals   1 2 3 4 5

Here you see the results of the customer focus self-assessment at InterTech (Table 10.7): some pretty large gaps exist between what the situation is and what it should be to meet the customer goals. Do you think the scores in your company will be wildly different? Try it out and see for yourself!

The difference between the actual situation and priorities at InterTech are clearly seen in Figure 10.4.

11

Phase II: Customer Marketing Analysis

It is one thing to bring together a bunch of facts and figures. Making sense of them is something else. In the analysis phase of customer marketing we try to make sense of the information we have gathered on customer value and customer behaviour.

ANALYSE CUSTOMER VALUE

1. Allocate margins and costs to individual customers and/or pyramid segments

This process always causes arguments. For instance, do you allocate overheads by revenues or number of customers? (We suggest allocating 50 per cent by revenues and 50 per cent by number of customers.) Allocation of marketing and sales costs per customer segments is also an issue. Remember, though, that customer-based accounting (CBA) is not the same as preparing an annual report for the shareholders or the Securities Exchange Commission. The idea is to discover information for you and your colleagues in marketing, sales and finance. (You will find that your controller or financial officer will become wildly enthusiastic about CBA, and will resolve many of the problems for you!) At the end of the day, you can come up with a cost allocation spreadsheet which looks something like the one in Table 11.1.

Table 11.1 *InterTech cost allocation per customer segment*

	Total	Top	Big	Medium	Small	Inactive	Prospects	Suspects
Non-customers	516					99	37	380
Customers	450	4	18	68	360			
Revenues	2,026,983	566,115	462,561	550,633	447,674			
Direct costs	1,183,484	339,529	276,039	322,228	245,688			
Margin	843,499	226,586	186,522	228,405	201,987			
Margin (%)	42	40	40	41	45			
General overheads	355,000	46,150	53,250	56,800	145,550	17,750	17,750	17,750
General overheads (%)	100	13	15	16	41	5	5	5
Sales costs	302,000	15,100	30,200	75,500	120,800	15,100	30,200	15,100
Sales costs (%)	100	5	10	25	40	5	10	5
Marketing costs	25,000	250	750	2,000	3,750	750	8,750	8,750
Marketing costs (%)	100	1	3	8	15	3	35	35
M&S overheads	70,000	3,500	7,000	17,500	28,000	3,500	7,000	3,500
M&S overheads (%)	100	5	10	25	40	5	10	5
Total M&S costs	397,000	18,850	37,950	95,000	152,550	19,350	45,950	27,350
Total M&S costs (%)	100	5	10	24	38	5	12	7

2. Analyse profit and contribution per customer and/or pyramid segments
3. Analyse ROI on marketing and sales per customer and/or pyramid segments

Having made the revenue, margin and cost allocations per customer (segment), figuring out the profit and ROI per customer and/or customer segment is fairly routine with a spreadsheet (Table 11.2).

Using this data, you can go on to extrapolate the value or profit generated by individual customers (Table 11.3).

While spreadsheets are great for the 'beancounters' of this world, you may want to disseminate your customer numbers to the rest of the company in the form of a customer pyramid. The results of InterTech customer-based accounting as presented to an 'all hands' meeting in the company cafeteria are shown in Figure 11.1.

This InterTech customer value analysis of profit and ROI per customer illustrates the key lessons learned from the customer pyramids.

- The top 20 per cent of customers deliver more than 100 per cent of profits.
- The bottom 80 per cent of the customers deliver a net loss.
- It is a good idea to move customers up in the pyramid!

ANALYSE CUSTOMER BEHAVIOUR

You have registered customer behaviour and represented this behaviour in the customer pyramid. Now is the time to analyse this behaviour, comparing behaviour from one year to another if possible. You need answers to these questions: how many prospects and suspects have become customers?... and how many 'active' customers have departed to the 'inactive' status?... how many customers have migrated upwards in the customer pyramid?... how many have remained in the same segment?... how many customers dropped down to a lower level? For this you need a migration matrix.

1. Create and analyse a historical migration matrix

You can build a historical migration matrix to show the dynamic changes of customer behaviour in your customer pyramid in

Table 11.2 InterTech customer value analysis per pyramid segment

	Total	Top	Big	Medium	Small	Inactive	Prospects	Suspects
Customer numbers	450	4	18	68	360	99	37	380
Revenues	2,026,983	566,115	462,561	550,633	447,674			
Production costs	1,183,484	339,529	276,039	322,228	245,688			
Margin (%)	42	40	40	41	45			
Margin	843,499	226,586	186,522	228,405	201,987			
Overheads	355,000	46,150	53,250	56,800	145,550	17,750	17,750	17,750
Result before M&S	488,499	180,436	133,272	171,605	56,437	-17,750	-17,750	-17,750
Sales costs	302,000	15,100	30,200	75,500	120,800	15,100	30,200	15,100
Marketing costs	25,000	250	750	2,000	3,750	750	8,750	8,750
M&S overheads	70,000	3,500	7,000	17,500	28,000	3,500	7,000	3,500
Total M&S costs	397,000	18,850	37,950	95,000	152,550	19,350	45,950	27,350
Operational profit	91,499	161,586	95,322	76,605	-96,113	-37,100	-63,700	-45,100
Analysis								
Customers (%)	100	1	4	15	80	0	0	0
Revenues (%)	100	28	23	27	22			
Marketing and sales (%)	100	5	10	24	38	5	12	7
Profits (%)	100	177	104	84	-105	-41	-70	-49

Revenue/customer	4,504	141,529	25,698	8,098	1,244	n.a.	n.a.	n.a.
Margin/customer	1,874	56,646	10,362	3,359	561	n.a.	n.a.	n.a.
Overhead/customer	789	11,538	2,958	835	404	179	480	47
Sales/customer	671	3,775	1,678	1,110	336	153	816	40
Marketing/customer	56	63	42	29	10	8	236	23
M&S overheads/customer	156	875	389	257	78	35	189	9
M&S/customer	882	4,713	2,108	1,397	424	195	1,242	72
Profit/customer	203	40,396	5,296	1,127	-267	n.a.	n.a.	n.a.
M&S ROI (%)	23	857	251	81	-63	n.a.	n.a.	n.a.

Table 11.3 *InterTech value analysis at the customer level*

Customer name	Last year pyramid	Last year revenues	Last year margin	General overheads	Last year sales costs	Last year marketing cost	Last year M&S overheads	Total M&S	Customer profit	M&S ROI(%)
Struckman Boards	Top	296,337	118,535	11,538	3,775	63	875	4,713	173,090	3,673
Unlimited	Top	143,945	57,578	11,538	3,775	63	875	4,713	81,655	1,733
Silicon Sync.	Big	42,365	16,946	2,958	1,678	42	389	2,108	11,879	563
Green Machine	Big	31,010	12,404	2,958	1,678	42	389	2,108	7,337	348
SpeedServ	Medium	13,659	5,600	835	1,110	29	257	1,397	3,368	241
Main	Medium	13,026	5,341	835	1,110	29	257	1,397	3,108	222
Sentinel Service	Medium	12,604	5,168	835	1,110	29	257	1,397	2,935	210
Colby Corp.	Small	4,791	2,156	404	336	10	78	424	1,328	313
Bates Milling	Small	1,717	773	404	336	10	78	424	-55	-13
Montpelier SA	Small	680	306	404	336	10	78	424	-522	-123
de Vries Inc.	Small	97	44	404	336	10	78	424	-784	-185
Bristol	Inactive	0		179	153	8	35	195	-375	-192
Wilkes Corp.	Inactive	0		179	153	8	35	195	-375	-192
Jones & Long	Prospect	0		480	816	236	189	1,242	-1,722	-139
British Techno	Prospect	0		480	816	236	189	1,242	-1,722	-139
Cellular Tel	Prospect	0		480	816	236	189	1,242	-1,722	-139
Bowdoin Bros.	Prospect	0		480	816	236	189	1,242	-1,722	-139

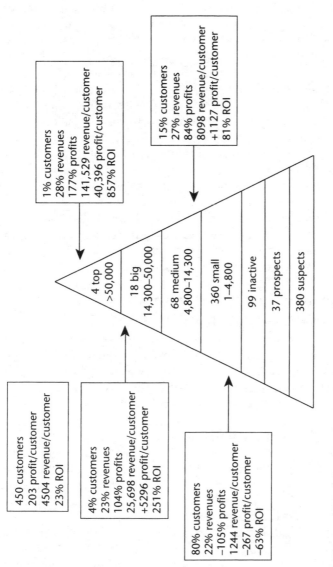

1% customers
28% revenues
177% profits
141,529 revenue/customer
40,396 profit/customer
857% ROI

15% customers
27% revenues
84% profits
8098 revenue/customer
+1127 profit/customer
81% ROI

4 top
>50,000

18 big
14,300–50,000

68 medium
4,800–14,300

360 small
1–4,800

99 inactive

37 prospects

380 suspects

450 customers
203 profit/customer
4504 revenue/customer
23% ROI

4% customers
23% revenues
104% profits
25,698 revenue/customer
+5296 profit/customer
251% ROI

80% customers
22% revenues
−105% profits
1244 revenue/customer
−267 profit/customer
−63% ROI

Figure 11.1 *InterTech pyramid: customer-based accounting*

the past year (or other appropriate time period you use for planning purposes). The InterTech migration matrix looks that shown in Figure 11.2.

Here you see exactly how many InterTech customers have risen in the pyramid (numbers to the left of the thick lines); dropped in the pyramid (numbers to the right of the thick lines) and stayed in their segment (numbers within the thick lines). At the bottom of the pyramid, you can also see the net result of changes per pyramid segment. For instance, there are four top customers this year versus three last year; 18 big customers versus 16 last year; 68 medium customers versus 61 last year and 360 small customers versus 375 last year.

The historical migration matrix is a useful tool for managers because the customer migration patterns can compare customer plans with actual customer behaviour in the past. In addition, detailed analysis of the customers which go up, remain static or go down in the customer pyramid can reveal characteristics which can be used to refine and validate total spend and customer share factors. This works best when you have migration matrices for two or more time periods.

2. Analyse total spend factors
3. Analyse customer share factors

There are two ways to analyse the total spend and customer share factors. First is the 'statistical' method whereby you make a linear analysis of the factors over a period of two or more periods and come up with a 'weighting' for each factor. Second is the 'educated guesstimate' method whereby you come up with a 'weighting' for each factor and calculate the results. InterTech combined both methods. They acquired the services of a student intern majoring in mathematics from the local university for the 'statistical' method and the InterTech marketing and sales people made an 'educated guesstimate'. The results of the two methods were then combined to produce the analyses shown in Tables 11.4 and 11.5.

As this book is being written, tools to help you make these calculations are being developed by Project ACUMAP (A Customer Marketing Pilot) which is supported by the European Commission. For more information, consult www.customer marketing.com on the Internet.

Table 11.4 *InterTech analysis of total spend factors*

Customer name	Last year total spend	Customer size code	Customer SIC code	Spend change (%)	Next year total spend
Weighting	*65%*	*20%*	*15%*		
Struckman	592,700	5	9	5	622,335
Boards Unlimited	202,700	5	9	5	212,835
Silicon Sync	529,600	4	8	4	550,784
Green Machine	34,800	2	8	3	35,844
SpeedServ	151,800	4	7	2	154,836
Main	13,000	1	6	2	13,260
Sentinel Service	18,300	1	8	1	18,483
Colby Corp.	110,000	2	5	3	113,300
Bates Milling	18,900	2	8	1	19,089
Montpelier SA	7,000	2	7	2	7,140
de Vries Inc.	4,600	1	5	3	4,738
Bristol	58,000	4	8	4	60,320
Wilkes Corp.	45,000	3	6	2	45,900
Jones & Long	158,000	5	9	1	159,580
British Techno	43,000	5	9	1	43,430
Cellular Tel	12,000	2	8	1	12,120
Bowdoin Bros.	3,900	4	6	2	3,978

Table 11.5 InterTech analysis of share of customer factors

Customer name	Last year total spend	Last year revenue	Last year share of customer (%)	Customer satisfaction	Main competition	Sales region	Next year SOC (%)
Weighting			*50%*	*25%*	*15%*	*10%*	
Struckman	592,700	296,337	50	4.2	Delta	Merlin	55
Boards Unlimited	202,700	143,945	71	3.7	Data B	Alice	71
Silicon Sync	529,600	42,365	8	2.2	Delta	Alice	15
Green Machine	34,800	31,010	89	3.3	Smit	Merlin	90
SpeedServ	151,800	13,659	9	3.8	Delta	Merlin	12
Main	13,000	13,026	100	2.7	Sole Supp	Alice	100
Sentinel Service	18,300	12,604	69	3.7	Delta	Merlin	60
Colby Corp.	110,000	4,791	4	3.5	Delta	Alice	8
Bates Milling	18,900	1,717	25	3.0	Smit	Alice	12
Montpelier SA	7,000	680	67	3.2	Data B	Merlin	20
de Vries Inc.	4,600	97	101	4.0	Sole Supp	Alice	10
Bristol	58,000	0			Smit	Merlin	5
Wilkes Corp.	45,000	0			Delta	Alice	5
Jones & Long	158,000	0			Smit	Merlin	5
British Techno	43,000	0			Smit	Alice	5
Cellular Tel	12,000	0			Delta	Alice	0
Bowdoin Bros.	3,900	0			Data B	Merlin	0

Table 11.6 *InterTech migration matrix*

	Last year	Top	Big	Medium	Small	Inactive	Prospects	Suspects
Top	3	2	0	1	0	0	0	0
Big	16	1	8	3	2	2	0	0
Medium	61	1	5	37	16	2	0	0
Small	375	0	2	22	312	39	0	0
Inactive	64	0	2	1	5	56	0	0
Prospects	37	0	1	4	8	0	24	0
Suspects	410	0	0	0	17	0	13	380
This year	450	4	18	68	360	99	37	380

4. Perform 'what if?' scenarios with a planning matrix

Having looked at your migration matrices and total spend/ customer share factors, you can now try out various 'what if?' scenarios with customer behaviour, ie 'What if we lose two top customers?', 'What if we migrate 5 per cent of our customers up in the pyramid?' The possibilities are endless.

Here is an example of a scenario at InterTech using the planning matrix to answer the question: 'What if the customer migration pattern this year continues as it did last year, and there are no changes in fixed costs?' The answer is given in Table 11.7: a profit increase of 106 per cent!

ANALYSE CUSTOMER SATISFACTION

1. Analyse importance versus satisfaction to identify improvement areas

A useful method to analyse customer satisfaction scores is the 'priority matrix', which balances customer scores for importance of a value proposition versus their satisfaction with your ability to deliver that value proposition. The 'priority matrix' segments your value propositions into four categories, each with its own message for that value proposition in that category.

- Important and weak value propositions. *Message: fix these now!*
- Important and strong value propositions. *Message: keep up the good work.*
- Unimportant and weak value propositions. *Message: fix these when you have time.*
- Unimportant and strong value propositions. *Message: are you overspending in these areas?*

See Figure 11.2.

2. Analyse loyalty indicators

At the same time, it is essential to analyse the 'loyalty indicators'. Are you the preferred supplier? Are your customers willing to continue buying from you? Do they recommend your products and services to colleagues and friends? (See Figure 11.3.)

While these scores are useful as benchmarks, InterTech was more interested in identifying those customers who were eager to recommend InterTech to others, and those customers who were most dissatisfied and likely to defect.

3. Identify unhappy customers

Of course when you measure the satisfaction of all of your (better) customers, then you can quickly identify the unhappy ones (or clusters) and start to prepare yourself to prevent their defection. At InterTech we can see a few unhappy customers in the selection (Table 11.8). Silicon Sync obviously has a service problem; and Main seems happy with the products but there appears to be something wrong in the relationship.

4. Select departments and people to join the improvement groups

Clusters of dissatisfaction usually become apparent, ie slow delivery, difficulty in reaching the account manager by telephone, difficulty in understanding the invoices. You should then identify the departments closest to these problems – dispatch, sales and accounts receivable – and ask the supervisor to nominate people who will be assigned to the improvement groups to eliminate the sources of dissatisfaction.

ANALYSE CUSTOMER FOCUS

1. Analyse gaps: situation versus priorities

Some analysis between the current situation and priorities concerning the customer focus factors is required. One approach is simply to rank the factors and look at the scores above and below average in the area of 'current situation' and 'priority', as shown in the InterTech example in Table 11.9. Here we see that the average situation score is 2.4, the average priority score is 4.2 and the average 'gap' between the two is 1.7.

2. Identify priorities for improvement in your organization, communications and information

You cannot fix everything at once. You have to set priorities. Thus you may want to set up a scheme like InterTech did to rank the priorities of areas to be fixed (Table 11.10). Each aspect is coded as follows to reflect priorities.

Plan results

Plan turnover	2,268,047	707,643	539,654	583,023	437,726	0	0	0
Plan profit	188,180	218,232	126,409	90,040	-100,602	-37,100	-63,700	-45,100
Plan ROI (%)	47	1,158	333	95	-66	-192	-139	-165

Change – absolute

Difference/customers	0	1	3	4	-8	29	-1	-28
Difference turnover	241,064	141,529	77,093	32,390	-9,948			
Difference profit	96,680	56,646	31,087	13,436	-4,489			
Difference ROI (%)	24	301	82	14	-3			

Change – (%)

Difference/customers (%)	0	25	17	6	-2	29	-3	-7
Difference turnover (%)	12	25	17	6	-2			
Difference profit (%)	106	35	33	18	5			
Difference ROI (%)	106	35	33	18	5			

Table 11.7 'What if the customer migration has the same pattern as last year and fixed costs remain the same?'

	Last year	Top	Big	Medium	Small	Inactive	Prospects	Suspects
Top	4	3	0	1	0	0	0	0
Big	18	1	9	3	2	2	0	0
Medium	68	1	6	41	18	2	0	0
Small	360	0	2	21	300	37	0	0
Inactive	99	0	3	2	8	87	0	0
Prospects	37	0	1	4	8	0	24	0
Suspects	380	0	0	0	16	0	12	352
Next year customers	450	5	21	72	352			
Next year other						128	36	352

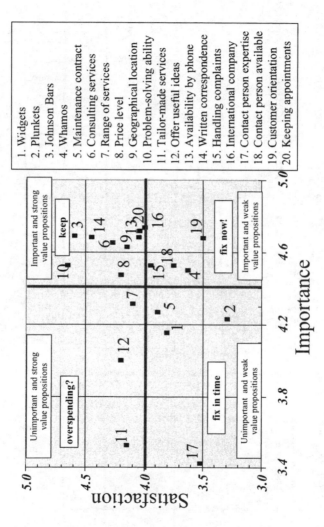

Figure 11.2 *InterTech priority matrix*

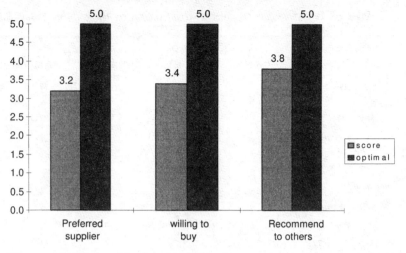

Figure 11.3 *Analyse loyalty indicators*

- Priority class A: priority score more than 4.2, situation below 4.0. Goal: fix immediately.
- Priority class B: priority score between 4.2 and 4.0, situation below 4.0.
  Goal: fix within six months.
- Priority class C: priority score less than 4.0, gap is more than 1.7.
  Goal: fix this year.
- Priority class D: priority score less than 4.0, gap is less than 1.7.
  Goal: Do not waste too much time on this.

3. Install customer focus improvement groups for organization, communications and information

Improving customer focus is an interdepartmental and 'bottom-up' process. Your customer focus 'improvement groups' charged to plan and carry out improvements will include representatives from all departments concerned. Some of the representatives from the improvement groups have already been identified after the customer satisfaction measurement. Representatives from other departments may be added.

How to manage the improvement groups? One option is to have the improvement groups managed by the customer marketing project group, with the chairman of each group being a member of the project group (Figure 11.4).

Table 11.8 *InterTech customer satisfaction at the customer level*

Customer name	Product quality		Service quality	
	Important	Satisfaction	Important	Satisfaction
Struckman	5	5	4	4
Boards Unlimited	5	3	4	4
Silicon Sync	4	3	4	1
Green Machine	5	3	5	3
SpeedServ	5	4	5	4
Main	4	3	4	3
Sentinel Service	4	4	5	3
Colby Corp.	5	4	4	3
Bates Milling	4	3	4	3
Montpelier SA	4	4	5	3
de Vries Inc.	4	4	5	4
Bristol				
Wilkes Corp.				
Jones & Long				
British Techno				
Cellular Tel				
Bowdoin Bros.				
Total	4.5	3.6	4.5	3.2

Another option is to have the improvement groups report directly to the management team/steering committee (Figure 11.5). In this instance, the supervisor of the department with the most direct involvement with the area may be the chairman of the group. For instance, the IT department is most involved with customer information and systems. (Some companies have successfully installed a primary IT user as chairman of the IT improvement group!)

InterTech chose option 2 and Table 11.11 shows how the improvement groups were selected.

Relationship quality		Preferred	Willing	Recommend	Total
Important	Satisfaction	supplier	to buy	to others	score
4	3	4	4	5	4.2
5	4	4	3	4	3.7
4	2	3	2	2	2.2
5	3	3	4	4	3.3
4	4	3	4	4	3.8
5	3	2	3	2	2.7
4	3	3	4	5	3.7
5	3	3	4	4	3.5
5	3	3	2	4	3.0
4	2	3	3	4	3.2
3	4	4	4	4	4.0
4.4	3.1	3.2	3.4	3.8	3.4

Table 11.9 *InterTech gap between current situation and priority*

Number	Item	Situation	Priority	'Gap'
1	Management is committed	3.5	4.1	0.6
2	Management sets an example	3.3	3.9	0.6
3	Management allocates (time) budget	2.6	3.8	1.2
	Organization: management	3.1	3.9	0.8
4	Know-how and experience	2.1	4.5	2.4
5	Customer focus attitude	2.1	4.4	2.3
6	People work in teams	1.8	3.8	2.0
	Organization: staff	2.0	4.2	2.2
7	Best method at lowest cost	2.2	4.1	1.9
8	Personalized communication	3.1	4.2	1.1
9	Benefit oriented	3.2	3.7	0.5
	Communications: methods/media/messages	2.8	4.0	1.2
10	Contact plan for every customer	2.3	4.5	2.2
11	Procedures for contacts	2.3	4.2	1.9
12	Customer-friendly communications	2.8	3.7	0.9
	Communications: contact logistics	2.5	4.1	1.7
13	Information is relevant	2.4	4.2	1.8
14	Information is complete	2.1	4.4	2.3
15	Information is up to date	1.9	4.3	2.4
	Information: customer information	2.1	4.3	2.2
16	System is effective	2.2	4.1	1.9
17	System is flexible	1.6	4.3	2.7
18	System is accessible	1.8	4.5	2.7
	Information: systems	1.9	4.3	2.4
	Totals	2.4	4.2	1.7

Table 11.10 *Setting priorities at InterTech*

Aspects	Situation	Priority	'Gap'	Class
System is accessible	1.8	4.5	2.7	A
Know-how and experience	2.1	4.5	2.4	A
Contact plan for every customer	2.3	4.5	2.2	A
Customer focus attitude	2.1	4.4	2.3	A
Information is complete	2.1	4.4	2.3	A
System is flexible	1.6	4.3	2.7	A
Information is up to date	1.9	4.3	2.4	A
Procedures for contacts	2.3	4.2	1.9	B
Information is relevant	2.4	4.2	1.8	B
Personalized communication	3.1	4.2	1.1	B
Best method at lowest cost	2.2	4.1	1.9	B
System is effective	2.2	4.1	1.9	B
Management is committed	3.5	4.1	0.6	B
People work in teams	1.8	3.8	2.0	C
Management sets an example	3.3	3.9	0.6	D
Management allocates (time) budget	2.6	3.8	1.2	D
Customer-friendly communications	2.8	3.7	0.9	D
Benefit oriented	3.2	3.7	0.5	D
Totals	2.4	4.2	1.7	

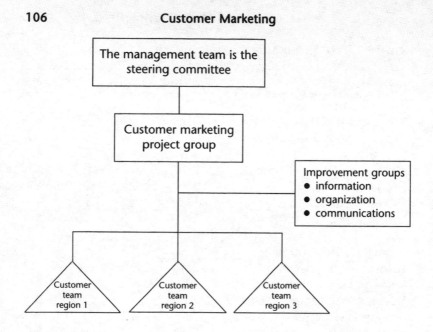

Figure 11.4 *Adding customer focus improvement groups (option 1)*

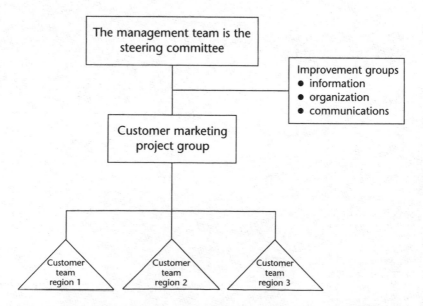

Figure 11.5 *Adding customer focus improvement groups (option 2)*

Table 11.11 *InterTech customer focus improvement groups*

Improvement team members	Customer focus domain	Specific aspects	Priority code
* P&O	Org–staff	Know-how and experience	A
* Works	Org–staff	Customer focus attitude	A
Council	Org–management	Management is committed	B
* Quality	Org–staff	People work in teams	C
Staff	Org–management	Management allocates (time) budget	D
* Management	Org–management	Management sets an example	D
* IT	Info–customer info	Information is complete	A
* Marketing	Info–customer info	Information is up to date	A
* Sales	Info–customer info	Information is relevant	B
* Service	Info–system	System is accessible	A
* Finance	Info–system	System is flexible	A
* Management	Info–system	System is effective	B
* Marketing	Comms–logistics	Contact plan for every customer	A
* Service	Comms–logistics	Procedures for contacts	B
* Sales	Comms–logistics	Best method at lowest cost	B
* Agency	Comms–MMM	Personalized communication	B
* Logistics	Comms–MMM	Customer friendly communication	D
* Management	Comms–MMM	Benefit oriented	D

12

Phase III: Customer Marketing Planning

Until now our customer marketing activities – registration and planning – have been pretty much a desktop exercise, often carried out within the marketing department. As we move to the planning and realization phases two shifts become evident.

- A shift from marketing to sales. When we start talking about exactly how much revenue can we expect from customer A and customer B, the people in direct contact with these customers begin to plan a more important role in the customer marketing process.
- A shift from top-down to bottom-up. We will see that customer marketing planning is very much a 'bottom-up' process. (But every 'bottom-up' process has been started by an enlightened leader who set things in motion through a 'top-down' approach and customer marketing is no exception.)

As the customer teams swing into action, the 'bottom-up' plans are made by those people responsible for them. InterTech customer teams were installed to serve the customers in per sales region. Each region had a customer pyramid which was consolidated into the company customer pyramid. The customer team members were the sales representatives for that particular area, the telesales person, the sales assistant who made appointments for the sales representative and the technical service person for the region. A marketing person (product manager) was assigned primary responsibility for making prospects from suspects.

PLAN CUSTOMER VALUE

1. Set top-down corporate targets: revenues, profits, market share, etc
2. Set top-down budgets for
- **methods & media**
- **customer benefits**
- **customer satisfaction programmes**

The planning process for a company usually starts with top-down budgets and plans covering next year's targets: revenues, costs, profits. These plans are usually developed from the wishes and expectations of the shareholders, tempered by the realistic expectations of top management. The management of a company which practises customer marketing should have real-world and customer-based scenarios to work from, such as the 'what if?' exercise discussed earlier. Because company plans for revenues, profits, market share or whatever will only be realized if there are sufficient customers and prospects with the potential to reach the targets.

As we see from the InterTech plans below, the management is going for:

- a 10 per cent increase in revenues
- no increase on direct costs since these are under long-term contract
- a 3 per cent hike in overhead costs due to inflation
- marketing, sales and marketing/sales overheads costs will remain except the 3 per cent inflation hike. Of course management expects that there will be a reallocation of marketing and sales costs since these will be planned on a customer-by-customer basis.

The marketing and sales budgets included not only marketing and sales methods and media but also 'customer benefits' designed to make customers feel good – and buy more! The 'top-down' InterTech budget made by the management team is shown in Table 12.1.

Table 12.1 *InterTech management team budget*

	Results last year		Top-down next year plan		Change (%)
Revenues	2,026,983	100%	2,229,681	100%	10
Direct costs	1,183,484	58%	1,315,512	59%	11
Margin (%)	42%		41%	0%	0
Margin	843,499	42%	914,169	41%	8
General overheads	355,000	18%	365,650	16%	3
Profit before M&S	488,499	24%	548,519	25%	11
Marketing & sales					
Sales costs	302,000	15%	311,060	14%	3
Marketing costs	25,000	1%	25,750	1%	3
M&S overheads	70,000	3%	72,100	3%	3
Total M&S costs	397,000	20%	408,910	18%	3
Operational profit	91,499	5%	139,609	6%	53
Customers	450		450	0%	
Revenue per customer	4,504		4,955	10%	
Profit per customer	203		310	53%	
ROI on M&S	23%		34%	48%	

PLAN CUSTOMER BEHAVIOUR

The customer team has the primary mission to plan and realize goals for each customer. These goals will be reflected in the customer pyramid of each team, and consolidated into customer pyramids at higher levels in the organization. The bottom-up goals are then matched with top-down goals. Normally some discussion and negotiation is needed to arrive at a consensus.

1. Statistical scoring per customer/prospect

While the customer team ultimately sets the goals for each customer, it can be aided by statistical scoring of each customer and prospect. You will recall that we estimated the total spend of the customer next year as well as the estimated 'share of customer'. By combining the two you will come up with a revenue target for each customer (Table 12.2).

Table 12.2 *InterTech statistical scoring*

Customer name	Next year total spend	Next year SOC%	Next year revenues
Struckman	622,335	55	342,284
Boards Unlimited	212,835	71	151,142
Silicon Sync	550,784	15	82,618
Green Machine	35,844	90	32,260
SpeedServ	154,836	12	18,580
Main	13,260	100	13,287
Sentinel Service	18,483	60	11,090
Colby Corp.	113,300	8	9,064
Bates Milling	19,089	12	2,291
Montpelier SA	7,140	20	1,428
de Vries Inc.	4,738	10	474
Bristol	60,320	5	3,016
Wilkes Corp.	45,900	5	2,295
Jones & Long	159,580	5	7,979
British Techno	43,430	5	2,172
Cellular Tel	12,120	0	0
Bowdoin Bros.	3,978	0	0

2. Contact scoring per customer/prospect

Parallel with the statistical scoring (often by the marketing department), the customer teams will also be making an estimate of what they think are realistic targets for each customer in the coming year. These estimates are based on the opinions of the sales person about whether or not the buyer is going to go for one deal or another – customer preference for you versus the competition – and general 'gut' feelings. Quite often, however, the sales person has a much better view than the statistician. For instance, the statistician may identify a customer which looks exactly like a 'top' customer but the sales person knows that the first cousin of the buyer works at the competition, thus making the 'statistical score' irrelevant. The InterTech customer team came up with the contact scores shown in Table 12.3.

Table 12.3 *InterTech contact scoring*

Customer name	Last year revenue	Last year pyramid	Target revenue
Struckman	296,337	Top	250,000
Boards Unlimited	143,945	Top	160,000
Silicon Sync	42,365	Big	110,000
Green Machine	31,010	Big	35,000
SpeedServ	13,659	Medium	40,000
Main	13,026	Medium	0
Sentinel Service	12,604	Medium	3,000
Colby Corp.	4,791	Small	20,000
Bates Milling	1,717	Small	10,000
Montpelier SA	680	Small	4,000
de Vries Inc.	97	Small	0
Bristol	0	Inactive	6,000
Wilkes Corp.	0	Inactive	0
Jones & Long	0	Prospect	10,000
British Techno	0	Prospect	10,000
Cellular Tel	0	Prospect	0
Bowdoin Bros.	0	Prospect	0

3. Customer team sets targets and goals for each customer/prospect

At the end of the day, the customer team sets the final customer goals and targets decisions for each customer, taking into consideration the statistical scores and contact scores. Of course, if the sum total of the target revenue varies greatly from the top-down targets, then 'further discussion' with sales and marketing management is usually necessary.

The InterTech customer team ended up with goals and targets which were negotiated with and agreed by the management team, as shown in Table 12.4. Having goals for each customer is fine – but what has to happen to ensure that the customer does what you have planned that he will do? What marketing and sales efforts will be needed to make the plan a reality? This brings us to the subject of contact planning, which is also a bottom-up event in customer marketing.

4. Set contact norms per migration matrix cell

An initial step to customer marketing contact planning is to set 'contact norms'. 'Contact norms' establish what marketing and sales effort is needed to migrate a customer from place X to place Y in the migration matrix. For example, what do you need to do to get a customer from the bottom of the pyramid to the top of the pyramid? And what effort should you expend on a customer at the bottom of the pyramid and that will remain on the bottom of the pyramid?

Two categories of marketing and sales effort need to be considered: 'methods and media' and 'customer benefits'. 'Methods and media' are the traditional marketing and sales activities: sales visits, outbound telephone calls, mailings, invitations to seminars and shows. 'Customer benefits' are those extra items which you offer to your customers to improve your relationship, such as the Christmas card (which nobody reads), the Christmas wine (which everybody drinks but does not remember from whom it came) and the Christmas dinner (which generally has an impact on those who attend). The InterTech customer contact norms for methods, media and 'customer benefits' proposed by the project group are shown in Table 12.5.

Table 12.4 InterTech customer planning as agreed by customer team and management

Customer name	Statistical score revenue	Contact score revenue	Customer goal	Target revenue	Target pyramid
Struckman	342,284	250,000	Keep	300,000	Top
Boards Unlimited	151,142	160,000	Keep	150,000	Top
Silicon Sync	82,618	110,000	Upgrade	100,000	Top
Green Machine	32,260	35,000	Keep	30,000	Big
SpeedServ	18,580	40,000	Upgrade	35,000	Big
Main	13,287	0	Downgrade	1,000	Small
Sentinel Service	11,090	3,000	Keep	6,000	Medium
Colby Corp.	9,064	20,000	Upgrade	14,000	Big
Bates Milling	2,291	10,000	Keep	3,500	Small
Montpelier SA	1,428	4,000	Keep	2,000	Small
de Vries Inc.	474	0	Lose	0	Inactive
Bristol	3,016	6,000	Create	6,000	Medium
Wilkes Corp.	2,295	0	Keep	0	Inactive
Jones & Long	7,979	10,000	Create	7,500	Medium
British Techno	2,172	10,000	Create	4,000	Small
Cellular Tel	0	0	Keep	0	Prospect
Bowdoin Bros.	0	0	Keep	0	Prospect

Table 12.5 InterTech contact plans per migration matrix

Plan position	CM goal	Sales visits	Outbound telephone	Business mail	Show invite	Christmas card	Christmas wine	Christmas dinner
Top								
Top	Keep	12	12	4	1	1		1
Big	Downgrade	8	12	4	1	1		1
Medium	Downgrade	6	9	4	1	1		1
Small	Downgrade	6	6	4	1	1		1
Inactive	Downgrade	4	4	4	1	1		1
Big								
Top	Upgrade	12	8	4	1	1		1
Big	Keep	8	12	4	1	1		1
Medium	Downgrade	6	9	4	1	1		1
Small	Downgrade	4	6	4	1	1		1
Inactive	Downgrade	4	4	4	1	1		1
Medium								
Top	Upgrade	12	9	6	1	1		1
Big	Upgrade	8	9	6	1	1		1
Medium	Keep	6	12	6	1	1	1	
Small	Downgrade	1	6	6	1	1		
Inactive	Downgrade	2	4	6	1	1		

Small								
Top	Upgrade	12	9	8	1	1		1
Big	Upgrade	8	9	8	1	1		1
Medium	Upgrade	6	9	8	1	1	1	
Small	Keep	0	4	8	1	1		
Inactive	Downgrade	0	1	8	1	1		
Inactive								
Top	Reactivate	6	6	4	1	1		1
Big	Reactivate	4	6	4	1	1		1
Medium	Reactivate	3	6	4	1	1	1	
Small	Reactivate	1	2	4	1	1		
Inactive	Reactivate	0	0	4	1	1		
Prospects								
Top	Create	12	1	4	1	1		1
Big	Create	12	1	4	1	1		1
Medium	Create	9	1	4	1	1	1	
Small	Create	6	4	4	1	1		
Inactive	Keep	0	4	4	1	1		
Suspects								
Prospects	Identify	0	1	4	1			
Suspects	Keep	0	0	4	1			

5. Calculate 'default mode' contact plans

Once the 'default mode' contact plans have been made for each cell in the migration matrix, you simply multiply the number of customers/prospects in each cell to estimate what marketing and sales resources will be needed to reach the goals. For instance, InterTech, as shown in Table 12.6, will need 752 sales visits and 2514 outbound telephone calls.

InterTech then compares the requirements with existing resources and discovers that the capacity for sales visits (1000) and outbound telephone calls 4000) meet the needs called for in the plan (Table 12.7). The management team subsequently approved the contact norms and the budget allocations.

6. Customer team consensus on contact plans

Just as with setting customer goals, the customer team ultimately decides how to allocate resources (sales visits, outbound telephone calls, Christmas wine) for each customer. Table 12.8 shows the InterTech customer contact plans established for each customer before the year starts. Of course there is room for changes and flexibility during the course of the year (but there should be no more confusion any more in the early months of November about which customer to invite to the Christmas party!).

PLAN CUSTOMER SATISFACTION

By now you will probably not be surprised to see that customer marketing also calls for a bottom-up planning approach to setting and reaching the customer satisfaction goals.

1. Set top-down customer satisfaction targets

Top-down targets are not exclusively financial. Top management should also determine top-down customer satisfaction goals. The top-down InterTech goals called for an increase to a minimum of 4.0 for product, service and relationship and also for the customer loyalty indexes (Figure 12.1).

2. Improvement teams propose satisfaction improvement programme plans for all customers

When tackling the problems of individual customers you will also come up with some programmes and solutions which can improve satisfaction and 'commitment' among all customers. At the same time, the 'customer satisfaction gurus' in the departmental teams will also develop customer-side programmes. At InterTech key plans include a 'zero defect' production programme with incentives; the installation of a 'service advisory board'; and a plan to roll out the customer interviews being done with dissatisfied customers to all customers in the top 20 per cent plus the high potential customers in the bottom 80 per cent and the important prospects.

3. Customer teams make satisfaction plans and goals for unhappy customers

It is essential to address immediately the problems of an unhappy customer. The last thing you can afford to have are ex-customers running around the marketplace badmouthing your company, your products and your services. They inflict great damage which you will never know about since the potential customers they scare away will never tell you.

You may not be able to make all customers happy all of the time. Even if they defect to the competition in the end, you should strive for the goal of having them say about you: 'They heard me out, they treated me fairly but we simply did not agree'. Sometimes you will discover that going out and listening to dissatisfied customers not only solves their problem but converts them into fervent evangelists for your company who proactively recruit new customers, proudly saying: 'XYZ company are a great bunch of guys, they use me as their adviser on consumer affairs!'

At InterTech, every customer scoring less than 4.0 in product, service and relationship quality was called to get more details on the nature of the negative score. Unsatisfied customers in the top 20 per cent – and the small customers with potential to move into the top 20 per cent – were visited personally by the account manager or other appropriate member of the customer team empowered to resolve the problem.

PLAN CUSTOMER FOCUS

1. Set top-down customer focus targets

In setting customer focus audit score goals, it normally makes sense to focus on one of the six clusters within the three

Table 12.6 *Default mode contact plans – customer base*

Plan position	CM goal	Number customers prospects	Sales visits	Outbound telephone	Business mail	Show invite	Christmas card	Christmas wine	Christmas dinner
Top									
Top	Keep	3	36	36	12	3	3	0	3
Big	Downgrade	0	0	0	0	0	0	0	0
Medium	Downgrade	1	6	9	4	1	1	0	1
Small	Downgrade	0	0	0	0	0	0	0	0
Inactive	Downgrade	0	0	0	0	0	0	0	0
Big									
Top	Upgrade	1	12	8	4	1	1	0	1
Big	Keep	9	72	108	36	9	9	0	9
Medium	Downgrade	3	18	27	12	3	3	0	3
Small	Downgrade	2	8	12	8	2	2	0	2
Inactive	Downgrade	2	8	8	8	2	2	0	2
Medium									
Top	Upgrade	1	12	9	6	1	1	0	1
Big	Upgrade	6	48	54	36	6	6	0	6
Medium	Keep	41	246	492	246	41	41	41	0
Small	Downgrade	18	18	108	108	18	18	0	0
Inactive	Downgrade	2	4	8	12	2	2	0	0

Small									
Top	Upgrade	0	0	0	0	0	0	0	0
Big	Upgrade	2	16	18	16	2	2	0	2
Medium	Upgrade	21	126	189	168	21	21	21	0
Small	Keep	300	0	1,200	2,400	300	300	0	0
Inactive	Downgrade	37	0	37	296	37	37	0	0
Inactive									
Top	Reactivate	0	0	0	0	0	0	0	0
Big	Reactivate	3	12	18	12	3	3	0	3
Medium	Reactivate	2	6	12	8	2	2	2	0
Small	Reactivate	8	8	16	32	8	8	0	0
Inactive	Reactivate	87	0	0	348	87	87	0	0
Prospects									
Top	Create	0	0	0	0	0	0	0	0
Big	Create	1	12	1	4	1	1	0	1
Medium	Create	4	36	4	16	4	4	4	0
Small	Create	8	48	32	32	8	8	0	0
Inactive	Keep	24	0	96	96	24	24	0	0
Suspects									
Prospects	Identify	12	0	12	48	12	0	0	0
Suspects	Keep	352	0	0	1,408	352	0	0	0
Totals		950	752	2,514	5,376	950	586	68	34

Table 12.7 Contact planning – capacity and budgets

M&S planning	Sales visits	Outbound telephone	Business mail	Show invite	Christmas card	Christmas wine	Christmas dinner
Capacity	1,000	4,000	5,650	963	500	77	40
Budget	202,000	100,000	11,300	7,700	1,000	1,000	4,000
Cost per customer	202	25	2	8	2	13	100
Needed	752	2,514	5,376	950	586	68	34
Cost	151,904	62,850	10,752	7,600	1,172	884	3,400
Capacity balance	248	1,486	274	13	–86	9	6
Reserve balance	50,096	37,150	548	100	–172	116	600

Table 12.8 *InterTech customer contact plans as agreed by customer teams*

Customer name	Last year pyramid	Target pyramid	Sales visits	Outbound telephone	Business mail	Show invite	Christmas card	Christmas wine	Christmas dinner
Struckman	Top	Top	10	10	4	1	1	0	1
Boards Unlimited	Top	Top	12	12	4	1	1	1	1
Silicon Sync	Big	Top	15	8	4	1	1	0	1
Green Machine	Big	Big	8	6	4	1	1	0	1
SpeedServ	Medium	Big	8	12	6	1	1	0	1
Main	Medium	Small	1	6	6	1	1	0	0
Sentinel Service	Medium	Medium	6	12	6	1	1	0	1
Colby Corp.	Small	Big	8	9	8	1	1	0	1
Bates Milling	Small	Small	0	4	8	1	1	0	0
Montpelier SA	Small	Small	0	4	8	1	1	0	0
de Vries Inc.	Small	Inactive	0	0	0	0	0	0	0
Bristol	Inactive	Medium	3	6	4	1	1	1	0
Wilkes Corp.	Inactive	Inactive	0	0	4	1	1	0	0
Jones & Long	Prospect	Medium	4	1	4	1	1	1	0
British Techno	Prospect	Small	6	4	4	1	1	0	0
Cellular Tel	Prospect	Prospect	0	1	4	1	0	0	0
Bowdoin Bros.	Prospect	Prospect	0	0	4	1	0	0	0

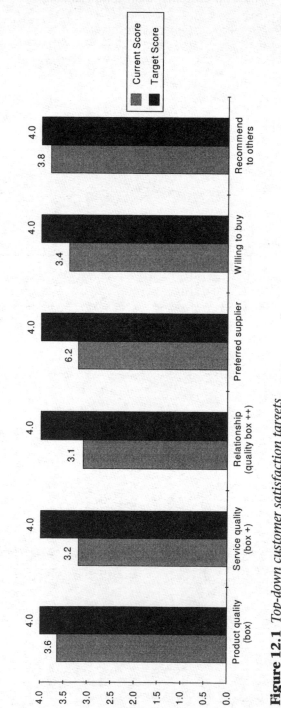

Figure 12.1 *Top-down customer satisfaction targets*

Table 12.9 *InterTech customer focus targets*

Customer focus factor	Situation	Priority	'Gap'	Target
Information – systems	1.9	4.3	2.4	3.0
Information – customer information	2.1	4.3	2.2	3.0
Organization – staff	2.0	4.2	2.2	3.0
Communications – contact logistics	2.5	4.1	1.7	3.5
Communications – media/methods	2.8	4.0	1.2	4.0
Organization – management	3.1	3.9	0.8	4.0
Total all factors	2.4	4.2	1.7	3.4

domains of organization, information and communications since improvement activities tend to impact on a cluster basis. It is important to use 'hard' numbers when setting targets for the rather 'soft' area of customer focus. Table 12.9 provides the InterTech customer focus targets.

2. Improvement groups make plans to resolve problems

The improvement groups are charged with making specific plans to resolve problems and improve customer focus. The InterTech improvement groups came up with these plans to meet priorities (Table 12.10). Note that where there is no priority, no plans are made!

Table 12.10 *InterTech customer focus improvement group*

Improvement team	Specific aspects
* P&O	Know-how and experience
* Works	Customer focus attitude
Council	Management is committed
* Quality	People work in teams
Staff	Management allocates (time) budget
* Management	Management sets an example
* IT	Information is complete
* Marketing	Information is up to date
* Sales	Information is relevant
* Service	System is accessible
* Finance	System is flexible
* Management	System is effective
* Marketing	Contact plan for every customer
* Service	Procedures for contacts
* Sales	Best method at lowest cost
* Agency	Personalized communication
* Logistics	Customer-friendly communications
* Management	Benefit oriented

Priority code	Customer focus improvement plans
A	Skill training for all front office staff
A	Customer video shows
B	'Call a customer a day' programme
C	Install customer teams
D	No action
D	No action
A	Undertake info inventory
A	"
B	"
A	Research external M&S package
A	"
B	"
A	Implement CM contact planning
B	"
B	"
B	Review all mailings and telemarketing scripts
D	No action
D	No action

13

Phase IV: Realizing Customer Marketing Plans

Until now we have been fairly detailed about the registration, analysis and planning phases of customer marketing. Now we come to the phase where you have to 'make it happen' – realization – and we have less to say about this phase except perhaps for some tips and sharing of experiences. Why? Because this phase simply entails management and staff commitment to carry out what has been discussed, planned and agreed in the foregoing phases.

REALIZATION OF CUSTOMER VALUE PLANS

1. **Progress checks for profit targets**
2. **Monitor expenses**
3. **Adjust/fine-tune as required**

Meeting customer value targets is the result of realizing all other business plans plus a healthy portion of good luck! There are no magic tricks here, it is just a question of monthly/quarterly financial reporting, taking into consideration the customer-related numbers of revenue and profit per customer, plus ROI on marketing and sales. The InterTech half-year financial reporting is shown in Table 13.1, which indicates that InterTech is pretty much on target for the year.

Table 13.1 InterTech half-year financial reporting

	InterTech plan/6 months		InterTech reality/6 months		
	Revenue	Revenue (%)	Revenue	Variance	Variance (%)
Revenues	1,114,841	100	1,123,458	8,617	1
Direct costs	657,756	59	660,939	3,183	0
Margin (%)	41%	0	41	0	0
Margin	457,085	41	462,519	5,434	1
General overheads	182,825	16	183,496	671	0
Profit before M&S	274,260	25	279,023	4,763	2
Marketing & sales					
Sales costs	155,530	14	154,729	−801	−1
Marketing costs	12,875	1	11,849	−1,026	−8
M&S overheads	36,050	3	37,653	1,603	4
Total M&S costs	204,455	18	204,231	−224	0
Operational profit	69,805	6	74,792	4,987	7
Customers	450		463	13	3
Revenue per customer	2,477		2,426	−51	−2
Profit per customer	155		162	6	4
ROI on M&S	34%		37%	2%	7

REALIZATION OF CUSTOMER BEHAVIOUR PLANS

1. **Progress check behaviour targets**
2. **Progress check contact targets**
3. **Adjust/fine-tune as required**

Since operational profits result from positive customer behaviour, reporting on these results run parallel to the customer value reporting. However, the big difference is the reporting at the customer level, whereby the customer teams can see whether or not they are on target for each individual customer, as shown in the InterTech report in Table 13.2. The prognosis is positive!

Customer behaviour is highly dependent on the amount of time, energy and attention paid to each customer. That means that the customer teams must accomplish the customer contacts and customer benefits per customer, as planned. The key is to get the visiting, telephone and mailing contacts in everybody's agenda at the beginning of the year. A quarterly or six-month check of what was accomplished versus what was planned is also essential. How this was managed at InterTech is shown in Table 13.3.

REALIZATION OF CUSTOMER SATISFACTION PLANS

1. **Progress check unhappy customers**
2. **Progress check departmental actions**
3. **Adjust/fine-tune as required**

Management must make sure that unhappy customers are dealt with properly; and that means reporting on the resolution of situations with unhappy customers to ensure that the issues were addressed. At InterTech, you may recall, customer Silicon Sync had service problems and customer Main was unhappy with the relationship. The account managers met with both customers, and both customers were pleased that attention was being paid to their complaints.

The management team, as customer satisfaction steering committee, should track progress on implementation of all customer programmes. At InterTech, realization of the departmental action plans also appear to be on schedule.

Table 13.2 *Customer behaviour realization check – six months*

Customer name	Customer goal	Agreed target		Target to date		Realized to date		Prognosis		Projection pyramid
		Target pyramid	Target revenue	Revenue (%)	Target revenue	Revenue (%)	Actual revenue	Prognosis revenue	Revenue variance	
Struckman	Keep	Top	300,000	47	141,000	57	171,000	330,000	30,000	Top
Boards Unlimited	Keep	Top	150,000	47	70,500	42	62,500	142,000	–8,000	Top
Silicon Sync	Upgrade	Top	100,000	47	47,000	46	45,553	98,553	–1,447	Top
Green Machine	Keep	Big	30,000	47	14,100	51	15,300	31,200	1,200	Big
SpeedServ	Upgrade	Big	35,000	47	16,450	24	8,400	26,950	–8,050	Big
Main	Downgrade	Small	1,000	47	470	50	500	1,030	30	Small
Sentinel Service	Keep	Medium	6,000	47	2,820	110	6,600	9,780	3,780	Medium
Colby Corp.	Upgrade	Big	14,000	47	6,580	43	6,020	13,440	–560	Medium
Bates Milling	Keep	Small	3,500	47	1,645	56	1,960	3,815	315	Small
Montpelier SA	Keep	Small	2,000	47	940	60	1,200	2,260	260	Small
de Vries Inc.	Lose	Inactive								Inactive
Bristol	Create	Medium	6,000	47	2,820	35	2,100	5,280	–720	Small
Wilkes Corp.	Keep	Inactive								Inactive
Jones & Long	Create	Medium	7,500	47	3,525	48	3,600	7,575	75	Medium
British Techno	Create	Small	4,000	47	1,880	59	2,360	4,480	480	Small
Cellular Tel	Keep	Prospect								Prospect
Bowdoin Bros.	Keep	Prospect								Prospect
Total			659,000	47	309,730	50	327,093	676,363	17,363	3%

Table 13.3 InterTech customer contact check – six months variances (0 = on target; – = below target; + = above target)

Customer name	Last year pyramid	Target pyramid	Sales visits	Outbound telephone	Business mail	Show invite	Christmas card	Christmas wine	Christmas dinner
Struckman	Top	Top	-3	1	0	0			
Boards Unlimited	Top	Top	1	-1	0	0			
Silicon Sync	Big	Top	-6	0	0	0			
Green Machine	Big	Big	4	0	0	0			
SpeedServ	Medium	Big	0	-2	0	0			
Main	Medium	Small	0	0	0	0			
Sentinel Service	Medium	Medium	4	-4	0	0			
Colby Corp.	Small	Big	0	6	0	0			
Bates Milling	Small	Small	0	0	0	0			
Montpelier SA	Small	Small	0	2	0	0			
de Vries Inc.	Small	Inactive	0	0	0	0			
Bristol	Inactive	Medium	-1	0	-1	0			
Wilkes Corp.	Inactive	Inactive	0	0	0	0			
Jones & Long	Prospect	Medium	0	0	-1	0			
British Techno	Prospect	Small	-1	-1	0	0			
Cellular Tel	Prospect	Prospect	0	0	0	0			
Bowdoin Bros.	Prospect	Prospect	0	0	0	0			

Table 13.4 InterTech customer focus improvement group reporting

Improvement team	Specific aspects	Priority code	Customer focus improvement plans	Six-month report
* P&O	Know-how and experience	A	Skill training for all front office staff	Training started
* Trade Union	Customer focus attitude	A	Customer video shows	In production
	Management is committed	B	'Call a customer a day' programme	Working well
* Quality	People work in teams	C	Install customer teams	In operation
Staff	Management allocates (time) budget	D	No action	No action
* Management	Management sets an example	D	No action	No action
* IT	Information is complete	A	Undertake information inventory	New fields in computer
* Marketing	Information is up to date	A	"	"
* Sales	Information is relevant	B	"	"
* Service	System is accessible	A	Find/implement M&S package	CM package found
* Finance	System is flexible	A	"	"
* Management	System is effective	B	"	"
* Marketing	Contact plan for every customer	A	Implement CM contact planning	Being used daily
* Service	Procedures for contacts	B	"	Being used daily
* Sales	Best method at lowest cost	B	"	Being used daily
* Agency	Personalized communication	B	Review all mailings and telemarketing scripts	OK, agency hired
* Logistics	Customer-friendly communications	D	No action	No action
* Management	Benefit oriented	D	No action	No action

REALIZATION OF CUSTOMER FOCUS PLANS

1. Progress check customer focus targets
2. Progress check improvement plans
3. Adjust/fine-tune as required

The realization of customer focus plans works in the same way as the realization of all plans. There have to be specific goals and periodic checks on their realization. At the six-month mark, the InterTech customer focus steering committee – in reality the InterTech management team – noted the results shown in Table 13.4.

$$\boxed{14}$$

Re-Registration: Closing the Customer Marketing Loop

Having gone through the four phases of customer marketing, you close the loop with a (re-)registration of customer value, customer behaviour, customer satisfaction and customer focus to determine what progress was made – and what lessons have been learned for improvement in the future. Let us take a look at InterTech after a year of customer marketing.

RE-REGISTER CUSTOMER FOCUS

A new audit of the customer focus factors revealed that InterTech reached close to 100 per cent of the customer focus improvement targets (Table 14.1).

RE-REGISTER CUSTOMER SATISFACTION

Good progress was also made in achieving customer satisfaction goals for all customers and at the individual level (Table 14.2).

RE-REGISTER CUSTOMER BEHAVIOUR

The migration matrix (Table 14.3) over the past year shows the detailed movement in and out of the InterTech customer pyramid. The net results can be seen in the graphical customer pyramid (Figure 14.1).

Table 14.1 *Improvement targets results*

Specific aspects	Priority code	Start score	Target score
Know-how and experience	A	2.1	4.0
Customer focus attitude	A	2.1	4.0
Management is committed	B	3.3	4.0
People work in teams	C	1.8	4.0
Management allocates (time) budget	D	2.6	4.0
Management sets an example	D	3.3	4.0
Information is complete	A	2.1	4.0
Information is up to date	A	1.9	4.0
Information is relevant	B	2.4	4.0
System is accessible	A	1.8	4.0
System is flexible	A	2.2	4.0
System is effective	B	2.2	4.0
Contact plan for every customer	A	2.3	4.0
Procedures for contacts	B	2.3	4.0
Best method at lowest cost	B	2.2	4.0
Personalized communication	B	3.1	4.0
Customer-friendly communications	D	2.8	4.0
Benefit oriented	D	3.2	4.0
		2.4	4.0

You will see a net loss in the number of customers. Forty-eight dropped to inactive status while new customers or reactivated old customers created a net customer loss of seven. Of course every company should strive for more customers; but with this InterTech example we want to dramatize the impact that you get from upgrading current customers. The InterTech customer behaviour results, summarized in Table 14.3 and Figure 14.1, are of course the sum total of individual customer results, as shown in our customer selection (Table 14.4).

Customer focus improvement plans	End report	Result score	% of target
Skill training for all front office staff	OK	3.6	90
Customer video shows	OK	4.2	105
'Call a customer a day' programme	OK	4.6	115
Install customer teams	OK	4.2	105
No action	No action	3.6	90
No action	No action	3.7	93
Undertake information inventory	New fields in computer	3.8	95
"	"	3.7	93
"	"	4.1	103
Research external M&S package	Selected package XYZ	3.6	90
"	"	3.9	98
"	"	3.6	90
Implement CM contact planning	Implemented	4.3	108
"	"	4.2	105
"	"	3.5	88
Review all mailings and telemarketing scripts	OK, agency hired	3.5	88
No action	No action	3.9	98
No action	No action	4.1	103
		3.9	97

RE-REGISTER CUSTOMER VALUE

Customer marketing – what is the bottom line? The financial controller was happy with the report in Table 14.5 and chart (Figure 14.2): InterTech had boosted profits by 85 per cent on a revenue increase of 14 per cent!

The InterTech employees put a chart (Figure 14.3) on the cafeteria wall to show pride in their ability to accomplish these key customer marketing steps:

- make a goal for each customer
- make a contact plan for each customer
- increase customer satisfaction
- improve customer focus

Table 14.2 InterTech customer satisfaction results

Satisfaction area	Importance score	Satisfaction score	Target score	Realized score	% of target
Product quality (box)	4.5	3.6	4.0	3.9	98
Service quality (box +)	4.5	3.2	4.0	3.9	98
Relationship quality (box ++)	4.4	3.1	4.0	3.8	95
Total	4.4	3.3	4.0	3.9	97

Table 14.3 *InterTech customer behaviour results*

	This year	Top	Big	Medium	Small	Inactive	Prospects	Suspects
Top	4	3	1	2	5	2		
Big	18	0	9	39	19	2		
Medium	68	2	4	19	295	44		
Small	360	1	1	2	8	86		
Inactive	99	0	3	3	9	0		
Prospects	37	0	1	0	17	0	24	
Suspects	380	6	0	0	0		12	351
Next year customers	443		19	65	353	134	36	351
Next year other		2	1	-3	-7	35		
Difference/customers	-7						-1	-29
Difference turnover	275,758	283,057	25,698	-24,293	-8,705			

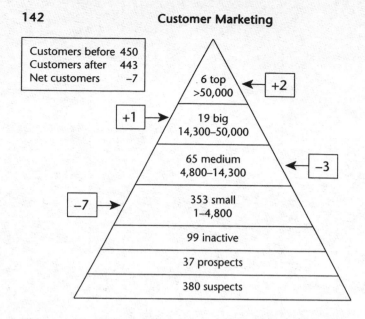

Customers before 450
Customers after   443
Net customers   −7

6 top
>50,000   ← +2

+1 → 19 big
14,300–50,000

65 medium
4,800–14,300 ← −3

−7 → 353 small
1–4,800

99 inactive

37 prospects

380 suspects

Figure 14.1 *InterTech customer behaviour changes*

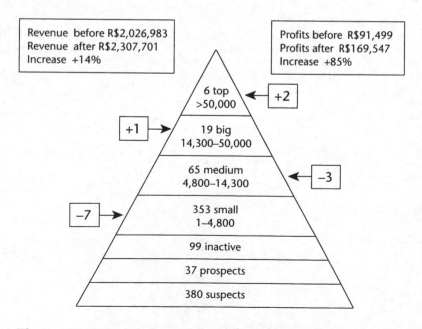

Revenue before R$2,026,983
Revenue after R$2,307,701
Increase +14%

Profits before R$91,499
Profits after R$169,547
Increase +85%

6 top
>50,000   ← +2

+1 → 19 big
14,300–50,000

65 medium
4,800–14,300 ← −3

−7 → 353 small
1–4,800

99 inactive

37 prospects

380 suspects

Figure 14.2 *InterTech customer value improvement*

Table 14.4 InterTech customer behaviour realization

Customer name	Statistical score revenue	Contact score revenue	Customer goal	Target revenue	Revenue realized	% of target
Struckman	342,284	250,000	Keep	300,000	354,647	118
Boards Unlimited	151,142	160,000	Keep	150,000	134,098	89
Silicon Sync	82,618	110,000	Upgrade	100,000	98,403	98
Green Machine	32,260	35,000	Keep	30,000	57,648	192
SpeedServ	18,580	40,000	Upgrade	35,000	76,298	218
Main	13,287	0	Downgrade	1,000	0	0
Sentinel Service	11,090	3,000	Keep	6,000	5,478	91
Colby Corp.	9,064	20,000	Upgrade	14,000	12,849	92
Bates Milling	2,291	10,000	Keep	3,500	7,638	218
Montpelier SA	1,428	4,000	Keep	2,000	3,728	186
de Vries Inc.	474	0	Lose	0	0	0
Bristol	3,016	6,000	Create	6,000	19,283	321
Wilkes Corp.	2,295	0	Keep	0	0	0
Jones & Long	7,979	10,000	Create	7,500	0	0
British Techno	2,172	10,000	Create	4,000	7,382	185
Cellular Tel	0	0	Keep	0	0	0
Bowdoin Bros.	0	0	Keep	0	0	0
Total	679,978	658,000		659,000	777,452	118

Table 14.5 *InterTech customer marketing results*

	Results last year		CM results		
	Revenue	Revenue (%)	Revenue	Change $	Change (%)
Revenues	2,026,983	100	2,302,701	275,718	14
Direct costs	1,183,484	58	1,358,594	175,110	15
Margin (%)	42		41	0	−1
Margin	843,499	42	944,107	100,608	12
General overheads	355,000	18	365,650	10,650	3
Profit before M&S	488,499	24	578,457	89,958	18
Marketing & sales					
Sales costs	302,000	15	311,060	9,060	3
Marketing costs	25,000	1	25,750	750	3
M&S overheads	70,000	3	72,100	2,100	3
Total M&S costs	397,000	20	408,910	11,910	3
Operational profit	91,499	5	169,547	78,048	85

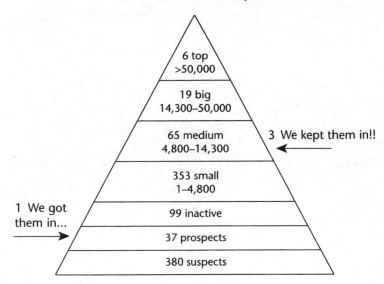

Figure 14.3 *Success through customer marketing*

Index